THE BRAND WEAPON

THE COOL STUFF TO BUILD LONG LASTING SUCCESSFUL BRAND FOR YOUR CAREER AND BUSINESS

GLENN LEE

Copyright © 2020 by Glenn Lee

The scanning, uploading and distribution of this book without permission is a theft of the author's intellectual property. The Cross-Linked Individual Branding model must be referenced to this book if you are using it for commercial purposes (non-profit applications). If you would like permission to use material from the book (other than for review purposes), please contact glenn.lee@t-labc.asia. Thank you for your support of the author's rights.

ISBN: 979-869-34-6870-2 (Paperback)

ASIN: B08KPHDC1M (ebook)

Acknowledgement

I like to dedicate this book to:

My Lord Jesus for all your strength and wisdom that lift me up time and time again.

All my LinkedIn connections and friends who have walked through this journey with me to build our personal brandings, thank you for all your support.

My beloved wife, Sarah, who is the constant reminder of God's love and blessings in my life.

All my friends I have made in my life journey, thank you. I am who I am today because of your friendship.

God bless all of you!

Content

1.	Introduction	8
2.	What is branding?	11
3.	Why do We Need Personal Branding?	17
4.	The Power of Social Media Platforms	22
5.	Content Writing Fundamentals	27
6.	Reach	36
7.	The Seven Principles of Social Media Content and Reach	42
8.	Lifestyle Social Media Platform Algorithms	44
9.	Professional Social Media Platform Algorithms	52
10.	Cross-Linked Individual Branding Model (CLIB)	70
11.	CLIB for Business & Entrepreneur Applications	84
12.	Developing your Brand Weapon	96
13.	Setting your KPIs	100
14.	Closing Words	104

1. Introduction

Introduction

The purpose of this book is to supply, in a simple layman yet joyful form suitable for anyone, clear guidance in the adoption and implementation of the entailed methodologies to achieve a successful and sustaining branding. If you are looking for answers on the above reason, you are on the right track. So, thank you for making this decision to pick up my book.

Unlike investment and self-improvement books, this book is going to be really straightforward, providing you all the essential information to build your own branding. When I wrote this book, I was aiming for just a hundred pages so that you can really digest all the information well without getting too overwhelmed or bored by the content.

I will start off defining the real meaning of branding and why you really need it before we go deeper. It is important that you get this perspective right or you will side track along the way. From there, I will touch on the social media platforms and trends, how it is different from traditional branding approach. I am going to share with you my seven principles of social media content and reach which is going to help in preventing you from making unnecessary mistakes in positioning yourself as a brand. Remember them well as you build your reputation.

Subsequently, you will learn about all the key algorithms in social media platforms to help you crack the system. This will be half the puzzle solved until you learned the Cross-Linked Individual Branding© (CLIB) model which is going to teach you all about creating long lasting and sustaining contents to build and establish your brand. Lastly, I will provide some easy guidance on how you can go about applying all you have learned. When you reached some level of success in your branding, please don't forget to mention this book.

An important thing to highlight is some of things shared such as the algorithms may be changed in the future as the digital world evolves. However, the fundamentals behind all of it will remain true for a long time. As you learned all these, it will help you through your branding journey ahead and you might even become savvier in learning the applications.

I believed this book is going to be an eye opening for you in many ways and no doubt you will finish reading it fast. The only thing that I request you to do is to take it slow and allow the information to be retained in you. Because you are going to rely on them as you apply them. You will know what I mean once you start your branding journey.

Ok, I am not going to be long-winded in my introduction. Let's cut the crap and start the ball rolling! Let's learn branding!

2.

What is Branding?

What is Branding?

When I begin to write this book, the first chapter has been a ponder for me. I am excited to jump into the things I want to share with you. However, the most important thing I think of before going into all that is to define branding clearly. Instead of going a big round and telling you all the success branding stories and taking up all the pages, overwhelmingly and exciting you at the same time, I'm going to be really straight to the point. Because the key to getting the whole branding right is understanding the definition.

Let's start with the bad news first, as I might have to shoot down some of the readers before having a big round of debates. Targets standby, here we go. Branding has nothing to do with your creative logos and hours of designing effort in artwork posters and advertisements. They are just like the branded clothes and accessories you carry; it makes you feel good but doesn't necessary attract business or career opportunities. Even promotion with a 90% discount still creates doubt on onlookers. They do play a part in building a brand but they are not the brand itself. Are you still standing? Good. Next myth.

How about a well-thought statement or slogan? Ehn't ehn't, not branding. How about things like Nike "Just Do It"? Ehn't ehn't again! I will talk about Nike and other sports brand later though. Some may sound nice and even cool, but if that is really branding, I will call my slogan "Buy it with no regret". I will define all these as wind chimes decorating your house, nice to look at, sounds pleasant to hear it every now and then, but after some time, you probably get used to its presence and almost forgot what it is there for. Statements and slogans are part of marketing which derives the values of branding. They may change over time but not necessary change the branding itself. Marketers sometimes failed to build branding because of these. They create a lot of wind chimes and make a lot of noise but people just don't understand what purpose they served.

Here is another big one that most people got it wrong. And that is believing an excellent product or service will be a good brand. Ehn't! ehn't and ehn't ehn't again! Ehn't ehn't ehn't! Tell me the names of the best household products you used at home that didn't make it to global success, you probably start looking at it now for a name. You may even have the problem to remember that name of an excellent service that you want to recommend to a friend. A good product or service leaves a good impression. But how each individual experienced that is different. Unless it is consistent, then it might become a brand name of its own. I will explain that soon but let me finish my rounds.

The last one is my favourite. How about putting my best studio photo as the main front to promote myself? Ehhhnnn't! But I see so many people doing that! Ehhhnnnn't! Did you notice who are those that are successful in doing that? They are likely TV hosts, presenters, celebrities, property and insurance agents where their personalities have been their branding front. Unless you are Keanu Reeves or Scarlett Johannsson look alike, don't even try. Have you seen a lawyer posting his photo to promote his services? It's probably a dartboard by now. Until you achieved a certain milestone in your brand, don't use personal photos, it will backfire if something failed and your mugshot is going to be one of google's favourite library for a few lifetimes. A bad branding is putting a front and trying to tell people who you are, and a good branding is sharing real values till the point that people are keen to know who you are.

"A bad branding is putting a front and trying to tell people who you are, and a good branding is sharing real values till the point that people are keen to know who you are."

A lot of time people tried to create identity to become a brand without putting a story behind it. Those painful efforts lead nowhere when people don't see anything beneficial for them. Then someone else came along with a less cool name and lousy design, selling the exact same thing but now it sells like hot cakes.

So, what is branding then?

It is the character and personality that people perceived to have a value intact for them to benefit. Consider it like a point of view of something subjective so that people can learn or benefit from. For example, sports brand like Nike and Adidas are always engaging famous sportspeople to be part of their advertisements. Their intent is to promote a sports attitude, a determine mentality, a healthy culture and perhaps, a nice physical appearance. This marketing strategy is to give people the perception of that particular sport brand. When a person wears a Nike, he is likely to perceive the value of wearing a sporty label. He is probably inspired to be sporty and by wearing that sweatshirt, trendy trackpants and finishing off with the latest track-shoes, he believed that others will see him as a sporty person. Little you know he is probably going to the nearby pizza place to order that extra-large pizza to go with his 6-pack abs, or more specifically, 6-pack beers. The slogan "Just do it" is just like a windchime to those themes, but now it rhymes well. For some, they wear it but they still can't do it. The user sees its purpose through his own perceived values.

A brand can also be a value that is emotionally or logically attached. That's why brand like Coca-Cola puts personalised messages on their cans and bottles, and when it comes to world cup, the national flags become the personalised cover. The drink itself is probably not the best-selling point to promote health value. By customising each packaging to associate with every individual, the consumers felt connected in a small emotional or logical way, their needs are somehow met in that way. Have you realised souvenir shops selling key chains with names on it? Some people will try to find their own names or the name of the person they intended to gift, that personalisation draws people. Image a car or a jewellery that customised your name tastefully on it, you probably consider it right?
That brings us to another perspective on branding. It can sometime mean competitive perceived value. Limited edition stuff drives people nuts. Some of the world records for longest queue is because of limited editions. Those brand names stuck in Guinness for life that even the future generation will find it hard to believe. On a smaller scale, it can again be a person's perceived value. If someone carries a watch that is only 100 pieces made in the world, he probably felt he is wearing something rare and made him different from others. The idea of uniqueness put him in a better competitive advantage. Well, even a one- and only-piece manufactured Casio watch by Audemars Piguet is going to be skyrocketed in price.

The bottom line of a branding is people must perceive a value and feel associated with it. Unless they felt a connection to that name, they probably won't do anything about it. This is the heartbeat of this book. Be it yourself or your business, I am going to show how you can establish your own personal brand that people will value. With well perceived value of your brand, amazing things can happen!

Are you still standing or have I knocked you off your chair? Shake it off and let's dance!

3.

Why do We Need Personal Branding?

Why do We Need Personal Branding?

In order to clarify that you bought the correct book, the next thing we must do is to clear this burning question. I want to make sure you finished reading this book and benefit from it. Why do we need branding? What purpose does it serve? The element of branding is to create a long-term sustaining impression and the connection that people feel comfortable with. It is like a label attached to a product, where people can get a quick glimpse of it and get an impression. The trick is to make that impression last.

So how did I come about starting my personal branding?

It all started when I was out of job for a period of time and decided to take up a class to learn about personal branding in LinkedIn with the hope of getting notice by recruiters. The instructor knows some fundamentals about LinkedIn algorithms which help to improve the view rates of posts. After that training, I begin to create my personal branding. At least at that point, that is what I thought I was doing. I was using famous quotes and writing a few liners to get attention. I tried posting technical articles related to my career background and also humours to spice things up. It was a desperate act, trying hard to get attention with nothing to offer. After a few months of trying, with no real results nor leads, I felt something amiss. Hence, I decided to take a step back and buy some books to read on branding. Two of the best books I have read are "Crush It!" By Gary Vaynerchuk and "60 Minute Brand Strategist" by Idris Mootee. From there, I went to the drawing board and layout my plan to build my personal branding. In fact, through the thought process, I have invented a branding model by accident. After strategising my branding weapon, I started building my personal branding in LinkedIn. Within 3 months, I have gathered many followers and after a year, I have close to 30,000 followers. That branding has also drawn many C-levels and directors to connect with me, even to the point of job opportunities.

Of course, like any normal person, I probably thought this is a one-off success. Hence, I decided to conduct a few free workshops and at the later part, some consultation services to some professionals and businesses. Those who followed the branding model reached great level of success. So, with many proven case studies and success stories, I decided to market this model into a book.

So, back to the question, why do we need personal branding? Allow me to share my story from a career perspective. I have three job loss in the past, and every time that happened, I went into a state of stress and start sending resumes like nobody business. It is like the most boring computer game where you keep shooting endless bullets till you finally hit the bonus round for an interview. After most of the interviews, I always pondered what I can actually do better to seize that job. But then I ended up shooting endless bullets again. It come to a point where I asked myself, a high achiever and reputable aerospace professional, with 5 patents at the age of 32, I am still trying to convince companies that I will be a great asset for them to have. Something is not right. These companies should be coming after me! But the question is, they don't know me. Rather than being convinced that I am the missing piece in the puzzle, they are finding any concerns they might have in my resume. Instead of asking how I achieved those results, they will ask why I left my last job. Instead of giving me a problem to solve, they will ask why I lose my job. Honestly, I feel like telling them if a company treat me well with a decent work life balance, expected salary, no stupid questions at work like the interview and an amazing boss, who want to leave? But I can't of course. I have to suck it up till someone appreciate my values.

Here is the point I'm making, how are they going to appreciate my values until they employed me? I'm stuck! And the scary part is what happened when I am in my late 40s or 50s and lose another job? They will judge my age instead of experience. Should I start my own side-line business before that happened? Then again, if I can't convince people to employ me, how am I going to convince others to patronise my business?

That's when I start my unofficial "PhD" research and self-graduated myself. I called it my Personal Hallmark Development. My objective is I want people to know me of my profession, my achievements, my background, my values, my beliefs, my character and my personality. I want them to come after me and offer me opportunities. I want to have choices presented to me to consider. I want them to want me badly instead of the other way round. They have to seek me out and hunt me. Rather than me thinking who is going to employ me, I choose to think there are companies stressing about how they are going to find a person like me. I want to help them gain the ability to see that in me in order to believe.

That's why you need personal branding. To create that long sustaining impression till the point that when there is a market need for a role, you are the first in their mind to consider. And it doesn't necessary apply only to job seekers. Even for businesses, you can't succeed without branding. That's how the social media is such a powerful platform to create awareness and reach. Talking about that, have you wondered how branding is done in the past without internet? It is a combination of aggressive newspaper and magazine advertisement, with creative TV commercial to generate that kind of awareness. If you keep seeing the same company name appearing everywhere you go, you are subconsciously being educated about the company. Together with good word of mouth, the brand is imprinted in your mind.

Taking this into account, building a brand is much easier now with the power of internet. It can be relatively cheap and, in some cases, free of charge. But the school of thought is the same: - you need two things, content and reach. Some people and businesses are very creative in creating contents, but their reach is poor. Have you come across some nice posters and interesting messages but can't even recall the name of that person or company? On the other hand, if you can have a good spread of network to reach out but poor in your content, it is going to destroy your reputation faster than you can create a brand. Content and reach go hand-in-hand. Either one is weak and the branding will end up unsuccessful.

In the following chapters, I am going to take you through on how to create sustaining content and achieve powerful reach. But before that, let's touch on the power of social media platforms. This one is stimulating, buckle your seat belts!

4. The Power Of Social Media Platforms

The Power of Social Media Platforms

In this digital era, if you are not aware, your life is revolving around it. Gone are the days where if you need to buy a specific household stuff, you go to the biggest mall and hope to find the boutique that sells it. If you need to learn something, you don't go library anymore, instead, you google it first and get some basic insights. Academic publications have even now permit online references like Wikipedia. When you want to read the latest news, you no longer trust a single newspaper source, but do your own search and read around the subject from various websites. If you want to get the best deal of an apparel, you don't ask around or go window shopping, you find all the possible online sources that sell that item you want, compare the price and shipping cost. By then, half your decision is already made to purchase it. When you want to know what are the upcoming movies for the year, you don't read magazines for that. Instead, you go into YouTube and get the first taste of all the trailers. When you have a particular health condition, you will search online to scare yourself before you see a doctor. The most amazing thing of all these is now you can even find your loss contacts online instead of just dreaming about it. Staying connected has never been that easy in the past without internet.

The digital world has definitely brought globalisation to a different level. People spent more time looking at their digital gadgets then watching the physical world in motion. They rely on their devices to carry endless tasks and remember a phone number almost becomes a chore. Answers are expected to be as fast as a microwave meal and delayed transactions are almost unacceptable.

No physical beings or non-beings are spared from this evolution. An old traditional café located at an isolated town can increase its business within weeks with good online marketing and charity communities can gain more support and donation with better transparency. Even a talented kid can just rise to stardom with a well performed online video.
So, if you are still looking for a career growth or running a brick and mortar business without an online presence, you are going to miss out a lot more in the years to come. Let me explain why.

Let's talk about some basic numbers.

Based on the Digital 2020 report published by WeAreSocial.com in partnership with Hootsuite, the number of people around the world (total population of 7.8 billion) using the internet has grown to 4.54 billion, an increase of 7% (298 million new users) compared to Jan 2019. Since January 2020, there are 3.8 billion social media users, an increase of >9% (321 million new users) since Jan 2019. In global context, there are now more than 5.19 billion mobile phone users, an increase of 2.4% (124 million) over the past year.

The average internet user now spends 6 hours and 43 minutes online each day. Global Web Index reports that an average person spent around 2 hours and 24 minutes per day using social media. Just a quick snapshot, I have selected the three most popular lifestyle and one professional social media platforms to give you a taste of the number of users.

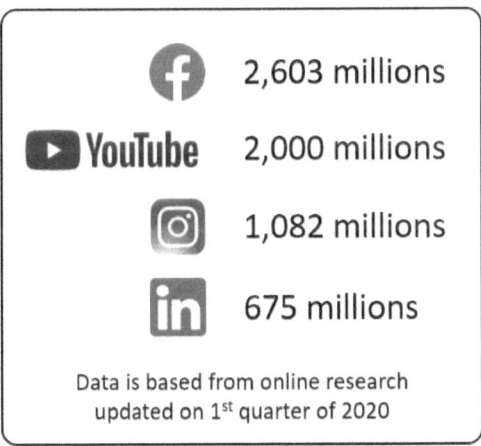

Figure 1 Number of associated social media users

Now here is a question for you: - How long is it going to take you to pick up the phone and talk to 1 million individuals and interest them about your professional background or your business? Probably the whole lifetime if you give up your social life.

On the contrary, you can maintain your social life and yet reach out to more than that. Looking at the statistical data of the social media users, there is definitely a big market there. Don't you wish you can have a small share of it? I'm not sure about you but I'm drooling just by talking about it.

What you really want to ask yourself is not how long it takes but how to do it. If you know the techniques, a lot of time and effort can be saved. What I am going to share next are not just showing you how to write and how to reach, but with a combination of that together with a proven methodology of my own creation, how to work smart and crave out a successful brand that sells.

Are you excited? Can't close the book right? Come on! Let's journey further!

5. Content Writing Fundamentals

Content Writing Fundamentals

Let's start with the more difficult topic, writing content. Some people find it easy, while others find it impossible. It is a matter of copying versa keeping it original. For people who want attentions, they will just keep posting all kinds of stuff to get attention. Basically, it is telling the viewers what you want them to read about you. It doesn't sound wrong, but in fact, it is very wrong. The approach is like going to a social network and keep telling everyone about yourself. The feeling is good and you felt your ego well boosted, but the surrounding people get tired of you. All they see is someone trying very hard to promote himself. Unless you are charismatic, rich and famous, people will just take what you said with a pinch of salt. Though some people will say, "I have people taking interest in me, they are actually enjoy listening to what I have to say." I don't disagree with that, because those people are usually less knowledgeable about the topic you are sharing and hence, taking interest in it. But what happened when they have learned enough from you? They will most likely stop listening to you.

That is the key thing about content. You must continually add value in your sharing. Not how you perceive it, but how others perceive it as values to them. Instead of telling people what you want them to hear about you, you should be telling them what you want them to hear about themselves. When they feel you are sharing things they can relate to, they will know you are listening to them instead of them listening to you. Can you see the difference?

Let's use an example. Say you are in the beer business and you want others to buy your beer. If you keep telling how good your beer is, people cannot relate to it. You can advertise the quality, the technology and the history behind it, but people will still see it as just another beer and there are many options of beers out there. Why pick yours? However, if you pitch your story from a beer drinker's angle, saying, "Are you thirsty for a good refreshing beer? Do you feel there is not a beer out there that can completely satisfy you? You are right. That's why this beer is meant for an avid drinker like you, because you know how to appreciate the good stuff." From this approach, you are letting the viewer or reader to decide, to see from their angles, to make them feel smart of their own decisions instead of yours.

I like this quote by Joe Chernov, "Good marketing makes the company look smart. Great marketing makes the customer feel smart." People don't like to be told to make decisions, they want to be the one to make decisions, or at least what they think they did. If you tell them what to do, their first hurdle will be questioning, "why should I believe you?"

Principle One – Treat your target market as smart people who can make their own decisions.

So how do you apply principle one? Consider yourself as one of them. Will you hire yourself? Will you use your own product or services? Why is that so? What makes you unique?

When you approach from this angle, you are speaking for them instead of speaking to them. But one might say, "How can I be like everyone? Not everyone will be like me." That's exactly the point. What you want is to first target the people who shared the common interests as you. You can't please everyone, but at least convince those who are like you. Until you realised this, you will end up writing contents all over the place to get attention from different kinds of people which, in the first place may never hire you or take interest in your product or service. You want to convince the beer drinkers to drink your beers, not the teetotallers or some monks living on the mountains.

The problem for those who went for content writing consultation and branding courses is they end up becoming more desperate in talking about themselves. If a person wants to get employed as a manager but keep talking about all kind of stuff, from raising economic issues to talking about poverty, from mentioning career struggles to sharing of jokes, people will wonder what values you can bring to a company. All they see is someone in a boardroom whining or trying to get attention. He should be talking about what kind of problem-solving skills a manager should possess, how to handle difficult situations as a manager and how to help organisations make money and be successful. If you are a CEO looking to hire a manager, won't his posts draw your attention?

Which brings to the next principle, "How can I keep writing so many contents? I can't write so much." I always like to address this question with the following example. If you ask a comedian to write a horror story, he will not last a page and after a few weeks, he will tell you he can't be a writer. But if you ask him to write about humours, all of sudden he realised he can be an excellent writer.

Creating a brand is like building a character and personality of something or someone but yet it has to be genuine. This is how others going to perceive that. For example, if I am going to write about how good looking, gentleman and generous person I am, would you believe me? But I believe myself! Nah... just kidding here. However, if I shared some experience about how to make yourself look presentable, give insights on how to show attentiveness and consideration to others and pointing out how to make a world a better place by caring for others, you will probably cultivate a perspective of what kind of person I am. If you shared the same heart as mine, you will draw attention to what I shared. You may even perceive how good looking, gentleman and generous person I am. At least this is how I made you believe. But honestly, we will come to a point that we can agree on that. Let's agree to disagree to agree.

On the other hand, if a person is plucking content from everywhere and sharing them randomly in his posts and marketing material, he is no different from someone in Facebook or Instagram who just wants to get "likes" and "comments". He will never cultivate a strong brand and adding to that, if a random person comes across his post which he is strongly critical about, the good impression is gone.

Principle Two – Position your content as such that people can relate to, feel beneficial in value and yet cultivate a strong good representative of you in their perception.

I will show in the following chapters a methodology that will help you develop your content endlessly. But before that, I want to share with you the third and last principle in content writing. This is imperative because at the end of the day, the purpose of creating a brand is to make people like you or your product and services. If you can apply principles one and two very well but end up upsetting the viewers, you are going to have problem rebuilding your own. Hence, this principle is going to save you before you get too carried away.

When it comes to content writing, never make it sounds very opinionated. You can share your thoughts and experiences but don't be too critical about it. Don't make it sounds like your way is the only way and everyone else can go to the highway. Allow me to elaborate further. Let's say you want to convince others to appreciate paintings and you want to teach people how to look at artworks. If you put forth a message like the following,

"When viewing a masterpiece, you should be looking at it from a distance. From there, you must find the angle where the artist captured the image. It is only then can you appreciate his work."

Does it sound like a message coming strongly at you? Is it telling you what to do? Because it is using words like, "you should", "you must", "only then can you". If you want likeminded people who appreciate artworks like you do, you are not going to make a lot of friends. Because others may have their own perspectives or preferences in looking at artworks.

Instead, consider the following message,

"When viewing a masterpiece, you may want to consider looking at it from various distances. Sometimes, you might find an interesting angle that may show the position where the artist captured the image. I have learned in several occasions to appreciate artworks from this approach."

You will realise I am using words like, "you may want to consider", "sometimes", "you might", "it may show", "in several occasions". The point is still put forth across but it now sounds like a suggestion instead of an instruction. Remember principle one?

You will also notice I used a lot of "you" instead of "I". One part of content writing is to involve people into the stories. Let them feel they are part of your sharing. It will make them feel more related. The other part is to avoid giving people the chance to put words in your mouth. When you used words like "I strongly believe", "This is how I do it", "I will", it is an invitation for others to challenge your thoughts. Most of the time, they can also be right in their own thinking. But instead of making them agreeing with you, you make them want to find areas to disagree with you.

Having said that, we do make mistakes when we write our content. There will be times where you may appear to come across strongly to someone even without intention. How do you handle that? Here's the deal, there will always be critics out there, much that you don't want to be critical, someone else wants to. They will choose to perceive something differently and put the spotlight on themselves. They want to steal your thunder. And if they are loud enough, they can actually take you down. My advice is not to make them feel wrong. The school of thought is if you keep insisting you are right, then that person will think he is wrong. And if you keep insisting he is wrong, then he will try even harder to prove you are wrong. It will be a never-ending journey and both of you will look like two fools juggling in the public. My suggestion is to thank them for their suggestions and taking the time to share their thoughts. Allow them to get credit for what they shared and they will likely walk away. If they feel offended in some ways, just apologise for making them feel that way. Never offend anyone when it comes to marketing yourself or your business. That argument will stick on you forever.

Principle Three – Allow the target audience to decide for themselves but direct them in a positive way. Never make anyone feel lesser than you.

Always try to consider these 3 principles when you prepare your content. Less of self, more of others. Because the contents are written for them to read about. Don't write contents for yourself and hope others will read. It never works unless you are writing your will. Moving on, let's touch on a few more principles. Don't worry, it is going to be less than the Ten Commandments.

6.

Reach

Reach

Typically, in the traditional way, a person's or business's reputation is built through socialising. A lot of time and money is being invested to build such relationships and gain support. This method doesn't grow old but it takes a lot of time. Challenges include convincing people to have the time for you, finding the right people to build relationships with, learning who are genuinely sincere in the relationship with you, how you can help one another and a lot more. It is not an easy work. Thanks to the internet, things can become more efficient especially in this fast pace microwave era. But bear this in mind, the internet doesn't replace the traditional way of building relationships; it only helps to improve the process of it.

Principle Four – The internet doesn't replace the traditional way of building relationships; it only helps to improve the process of it.

By understanding this, it will help you identify the right approach and intention of reaching out and widening your network. So, before you go all over the place shoving pamphlets to everyone in your path, think about who are your target audience. If you are selling household stuff, who are the likely buyers? If your answer is housewives, that is not thorough enough. In modern context, husbands also help with housework and they also want to make it easy for themselves. How about the kids? They can also be involved. So, household stuff is likely for anyone who stays in a house. That understanding helps in better positioning of yourself to that market.

How about job seekers? You have to think about what job and industry you want to get into. Once you decided on that, your target audience will be the senior management and human resource of that industry. Even the head-hunters specialised in that industry are also your target audience. If you are specified about the location of where you want to work at, then you have to narrow down your target audience. Although the target is smaller now, you are also more focus on what you want. Your target has become a likely catchment area.

It sounds simple but it is not, I have to be honest with you. Before you launched your content, you need to know who will be reading them. It is all about doing enough research to identify who you want to get attention from. Sometimes you may also need to adjust your content slightly to improve the reach to your focus group. Remember this, generalised effort only leads to generalised results. What you really want is to keep hitting the bullseye regularly.

Principle Five – Identify your key target audiences to gain the right applauds. Not everyone appreciates the same song.

You might be wondering why principle five doesn't come first as principle one. The reason is that you have to write your content genuinely from your style and character. Then you can decide who might be interested. If you pick the audience first before you choose your song, you might not be performing at your best abilities. Identify your talents first and then choose your performing stage. Recognise yourself before seeking recognition. Never compromise your talents for the wrong audience.

Principle Six – Recognise yourself before seeking recognition.

Now that you understand principles 1 to 6, here is the fun part: - learning the algorithms of the social media platforms. I will be emphasising on two platforms, namely, LinkedIn and Facebook. If you are a professional or a business owner, LinkedIn is considered the associated platform for your reach. It is commonly known as the professional social media platform, so treat it professionally, not casually like Facebook. Which means you are not supposed to post anything you like such as your daily meals or your personal lifestyles. If you are a self-starter of a business related to lifestyles such as holidays, food & beverages, hobbies, gardening, etc., then Facebook is considered the better platform for your reach. I considered it as the lifestyle social media platform. Most platforms fall into the lifestyle categories as it is more profitable with larger and more interesting topics. To date, I know there are more than 50 lifestyle social media platforms, such as Instagram, Tumblr, Spaces, etc. You have to decide which platforms work best for you. For my advice, it is good to focus on one platform and build success on it before you try another one. For training purposes, I will just use Facebook to represent the lifestyle social media platform in discussing the algorithms.

Which brings me to the last Principle. Last one I promised.

Principle Seven – Observe your audiences' responses and keep driving their interest.

When I worked as a DJ during my early career, apart from having the knowledge of music and able to mix them well, one of the most important skills is observation. If you just play music you enjoy, you may end up driving the crowd away. Hence, I have to observe the mood of the crowd, how big they are, how much they have drank, and importantly, are they really enjoying the music by dancing and are they expressing it. You don't pump up the music when there is no response, it will sound like a loud untalented stage rehearsal in an empty space instead of a real party. From there, I have to build the tempo and momentum, create the energy and drive them wild. In that way, they will burn out their energies, keep buying drinks to refresh themselves and get high. The club owners will be happy because of good sales, and I will get to keep promoting my style of music.

Likewise, in social media platforms, you don't want to talk about cars today and aeroplanes tomorrow. If you talk about cars, observe what they like to discuss about cars. Is it the engine, the design, the performance, etc.? Drive that interest further so that they will keep participating in your contents. With the right angle, you can actually drift away in talking about aeroplanes tactfully. Find the similarities like the engines and build another interest category of topics. People are always demanding, just like my party crowd. I can't just play pop music whole night. A bit of rock, heavy metal, trances and sometimes slow melodies all come into play when the mood is right. I have to be prepared to ensure those songs are available. You just need to learn the right timing.

On more key thing before we proceed further. Take note the main difference between Facebook and LinkedIn is that people in Facebook doesn't usually enjoy contents that are too "seriously corporate" while people in LinkedIn doesn't appreciate contents that are too "seriously personal lifestyle".

I can't emphasise on this enough.

I like to use music to explain that again. You don't go into a jazz bar, light up a cigar and enjoy a glass of wine to listen to pop music. I am not saying pop music is poop music. I am saying that everything has its right place. People goes to jazz bar to listen to jazz, if they want pop music, they will go to another club, don't spoil the cigar and wine! The funny thing is if that jazz bar insists on keep playing pop music, guess what? People will not keep complaining, they will just walk away and find another jazz bar. What will happen to that Jazz Poop Bar? I think you know.

I have witnessed many times people trying to discuss too much stuff about work on Facebook while another group trying to show their lunch and selfies on LinkedIn. These groups should come together and exchange their seats. No one will tell them it is not interesting. They will just choose to ignore and unfollow them. Remember this, most people have both Facebook and LinkedIn accounts. Which means they know the difference and why they have to keep the accounts separately.

Ok enough of that, let's talk algorithms!

7.

The Seven Principles Of Social Media Content and Reach

The Seven Principles of Social Media Content and Reach

For your easy reference.

Principle One
Treat your target market as smart people who can make their own decisions.

Principle Two
Position your content as such that people can relate to, feel beneficial in value and yet cultivate a strong good representative of you in their perception.

Principle Three
Allow the target audience to decide for themselves but direct them in a positive way. Never make anyone feel lesser than you.

Principle Four
The internet doesn't replace the traditional way of building relationships; it only helps to improve the process of it.

Principle Five
Identify your key target audiences to gain the right applauds. Not everyone appreciates the same song.

Principle Six
Recognise yourself before seeking recognition.

Principle Seven
Observe your audiences' responses and keep driving their interest.

8. Lifestyle Social Media Platform Algorithms

Lifestyle Social Media Platform Algorithms

To begin, I have to declare what I am sharing here is not rocket science. If you spent enough time researching, you will find as much information as the following. The only difference is I have done all the research work and tested them over the years so that you don't have to, making your life a lot easier. However, it is worthy to do some research of your own and learn more. You never know you may find something I have yet to discover or mention in this book. Adding to that, with growth in social media users and contents, the algorithms will evolve over time and it is good to keep up to date with the trend of the social media you are using.

Let's start with Facebook algorithms. When Facebook first started in 2004, it was a platform solely to connect and interact with people. As the membership increases exponentially, the style of communication also evolves. Hence, the newsfeed was introduced in 2006 to enable better engagement through posts. The "like" function was invented in 2007 and since then, some people's lives begin to revolve crazily around that. But it was only 2009 that the algorithms were created. The purpose of the algorithms is to create a sorting system on how every user's personal newsfeed will look like. Why is that important?

Imagine this, you wake in the morning, sitting at the dining table enjoying your breakfast and looking through the daily newspaper. You are not likely to read all the news, but flipping the pages to find news that you are interested in or matter to you. If nothing really worth a read, you will be done with the newspaper in minutes, then telling yourself a complete waste of money buying the newspaper.

That's why Facebook studies the behaviour of how you engage in the newsfeed. If you are interested in a particular friend's activities, you will tend to spend more time reading his posts, like and give comments. You will probably tag him when you want to share a common interest or a photo together. As you do this regularly, you will realise that friend's latest posts will be prioritised in your newsfeed. This is to keep you entertained reading the newsfeed of everyone's news that matters to you. Same principle applies when you decide to follow an interest group.

Do you have connections which you don't associate very well with or don't really like his type of posts? You will realise if you don't engage much of his posts, it will fall in the pecking order of your newsfeed. Unless you scroll really long down in the newsfeed, you will probably miss it.

This sorting system aims to make you spend more time enjoying Facebook. And the more time you spent, the more you will come across advertisements, promotions and other marketing stuff. Like a newspaper with some promotion or discount cut-outs, you can also save or bookmark those adverts for future consideration. This is how the business comes in. But of course, those adverts need to have a good reach too right? So, Facebook offered customised paid services to increase your reach, which is a form of advertisement services. On the other hand, there are also people being paid to like your posts so as to improve the view rates. These people are paid to do only that and they are not necessary interested. The objective is that when you see a post with high number of likes, there is a tendency you might check it out too. You can google online for such services but I don't really encourage it. Because if you have poor content and yet a high view rate, it is a giveaway for a paid service.

Now that you understand this concept, how do you get the algorithms to work for you?

Let's talk about how to improve your personal Facebook postings first. To gain support of likes and comments, you must first give before you receive. Be genuine interested in others' posts. Like and comment their posts. If possible, select other positive reactions such "haha", "wow" or "love". In simple, be engaging. Just as the algorithms assess the type of reactions and meaningful interactions you have in your engagements, your connections will do the same assessment about you subconsciously. If you have been taking interest in them, they will reciprocate as well. They will also like and comment on your posts. When they comment on your posts, engage them further by responding to their comments. Keep it going. The more you do that, the higher priority it will become in your connections' newsfeed. Even for those who hardly engage with you will also see your posts going to the top in their newsfeed. Eventually you will top your own ranking in your Facebook connections.

Of course, there will always be some people who are only interested in posting their own stuff but not engaging with others. Typically, you will realise they don't receive much responses. The common question people asked if you support their posts. Personally, I do. If it is a nice post worthy to comment, I will give my support. However, if the person never responds or taking interest in my posts after some time, I will take it as he is self-centred and I shouldn't be bothered. But hey, at least I tried as a friend.

An important note matter to my heart. If you want to have a good image in Facebook, then take this advice from me. If you have nothing good to say, then don't say anything. You can be humorously sarcastic but don't go into arguments or leave critical opinions on any posts. When people start to see a lot of negativity in your posts, there is a possibility they will unfollow you. If that happens, there is a very slim chance they will follow you back again. People hardly check on profiles they lose interest to decide if they want to follow back. The worst thing is that you don't even know your profile has been unfollowed. Hence, your popularity increases with positivity but negativity can decrease it almost permanently.

The personal Facebook popularity is easy to achieve. But how about a business Facebook page? That is a lot more efforts. Imagine doing all the above in your Personal Facebook account, but now you have to join a likeminded interest group or page and do the same. To make it slightly easy, find a group that has big number of members. Personally, any group with more than 20,000 members is a good size. Be active in that group but don't rush into postings once you joined. Be engaging first for at least two weeks so that people can appreciate your support in their posts. In that way, they start to get familiar and comfortable with you. Thereafter, you can submit your own posts and engage further.

Did I mention the above is just the first step? Once you earn your strips, there will be people who subconsciously becomes your followers. If you are really active in that group for at least a month, you can now form your own business group or page and invite this group of people to join. These people are now your potential target audience. They will also start to invite people to join. But if you want to grow your members bigger, you have to repeat the process. Find another group and repeat the steps. Typically, you need to grow to around 20,000 members or more to really enjoy good business support.

One typical question people asked, "why do I need to create a separate group page? Why can't I use my existing personal profile to build my business?" There are two reasons for that. Firstly, you need to keep personal affairs separate from business dealings. If your business doesn't turn up well, your personal image may suffer as a result. Secondly, a personal Facebook account allows a maximum of 5,000 connections but a page can have unlimited number of followers. Another shortcut is to create another personal account but associate that profile with your business only. Use this account to connect to as many people as possible that is not related to your personal life. These people will be willing to link up because they are likely to be in the online business as well. You can easily build the numbers and add them to your business group. But bear in mind this shortcut is just to build the member numbers of your group only.

All the above may sound a lot to take in. So, allow me to give you a step-by-step summary.

Personal Facebook Reach

Step 1 – Always be engaging in other people posts before you want to receive.

Step 2 – When your connections return the favour in your posts, engage them further in their comments.

Business Facebook Reach

Step 1 – Before you start your own business group or page, join a similar group or page first. Find a group with more than 20,000 members if possible.

Step 2 – Engage in people's posts actively.

Step 3 – Do step 2 for at least 2 weeks to get yourself noticed.

Step 4 – Start submitting your own posts and engage further, but don't neglect step 2.

Step 5 – Wait for at least a month doing steps 2 and 4 before forming your own business group or page.

Step 6 – Invite the current members in the group you are following to your own group / page.

Step 7 – Repeat all the above to grow your group members.

Does the above sound easy enough? It does require a lot of time and effort. Though in this internet era, the connections and reach are far easier and faster than the traditional way. If you are serious in growing your online business presence, this is the fastest way to create awareness and building a brand.

For business group or page, Facebook has an insights function that show the performance of your page. It shows where are the areas that are doing well and which one needs to work on. Personally, I feel at the end of the day, those results must convert to business returns. Hence, once you can grow your group or page to more than 20,000 followers, I believe you will see some tangible results.

Another thing to note and you will realise later in the professional social media platform that it is more vital in regards to the respond rate. When a post is uploaded, the algorithms start to trigger how much attention it is getting. The first few hours are the most critical. The more people respond to it, the more it will rise up in ranking on the newsfeed of your connections. If you are doing a public post, this becomes important. Hence, the more connections you have, the better chances of getting more and faster responses. Sharing of your post by others also help to extend that reach. The only problem is sometimes viewers respond to the shared post instead of the original. Hence, it may not be as effective.

If your post is constantly getting responses per minute and increasingly exponentially, it is likely to go viral. This can last for weeks especially on YouTube platform. The challenging part is to maintain that upward responses. Hence, eventually it will wear off and fall in pecking order for other new posts. Some people has tried to beat this algorithm by sharing the link of their posts on other social platforms so as to draw new viewers. However, some platforms have now realised this is not healthy when people are drawn away from their platforms. Some social media platforms try to reprogram the link to a different name upon posting or add a different algorithm to a post with an external link so that it is harder to increase its reach. Facebook on the other hand encourages that and have bought over Instagram and WhatsApp to increase the reach to their advantages. Their combined platforms have more than 5 billion users around the world.

If you want to go global with your lifestyle business, imagine such platforms can help you extend your reach so much if you know how to put forth good contents and take advantage of the algorithms. Imagine 2 billion of active Facebook users and you managed to only attract 0.0001% or 2,000 users to be interested in your products or services per month. Each of them just paying you a dollar for that. That is $2,000 income per month! Think about it. That is the power of internet and social media!

No wonder social media engagement can easily become more than a full-time job as it is always running 24/7. That's the best part, you can even make money while you are sleeping when people are still engaging on your online page.

9. Professional Social Media Platform Algorithms

Professional Social Media Platform Algorithms

When it comes to professional social media platform such as LinkedIn, it is a lot trickier. Unlike lifestyle social media platforms, no one care about your personal lifestyles or what you do in your career. Everyone cares about their own affairs and how to boost their careers. Not much of a social media isn't it? Don't believe me so, let's do a litmus test. Pick anyone with a profile of around 1,000 followers and who post on a few occasions. Look at his record and you will realise they received very low or no response. 1,000 followers are almost double a typical Facebook profile's number of connections. Yet the level of engagement is much higher in Facebook. Sad isn't it? No one cares about each other in LinkedIn.

Well, I said they don't care but I didn't say they won't be interested. Hence, the 7 principles applied even more significantly in LinkedIn. Adding to that, there are strategies to build that interest. But before we go into that, let's talk about its algorithms.

Over the years, the LinkedIn has been evolving its algorithms but slower in the likes of lifestyle social media platforms such as Facebook. In the past, LinkedIn's algorithm has allowed some popular profiles to translate their posts easily to viral. These are given the celebrity or the official, influencer status. This creates an imbalance where average users do not get much of an attention. Although the algorithms have improved, the "culture" will take quite some time to change. Just like Facebook, LinkedIn also has a sorting system. It comprises of 7 factors:

1. Connections and Followers
2. Common Interests
3. Engagement Rate
4. Golden Hour
5. Timing of Post
6. View Rate Data and Social Selling Index (SSI)
7. Social Sharing

The sorting system determines three outcomes: - How it will prioritise your posts, how it will rank your profile during search and how it will promote your content for engagement.

By knowing all these, you will know which angle to work on. Let's dive deeper into these factors and learn how to optimise it.

1. Connections and Followers

LinkedIn allows up to 30,000 1st level connections in your account. That is the limit but compared to Facebook personal account of 5,000, that is a lot. But why do we need so many connections?

Because your reach depends on it. Allow me to explain further.

Let's say Michael is connected to Francis, so they are 1st level connection to each other. And Francis is connected to Simon but Simon is not connected to Michael. So, Simon is Francis' 1st level and Michael's 2nd level. Then Travis comes along and connected to Simon but not connected to the rest. Travis is Simon's 1st, Francis' 2nd and Michael's 3rd connection. Now if someone like Felicia who is a new member that joined LinkedIn and is connected to Travis and not the rest, she will be significantly "out of radar" from Michael. Unless Michael and Felicia know each other specifically by name, company or email, they are considered out of range from each other in normal circumstances. I said normal unless either one of them have a post that went viral, they will not have discovered each other for a long time. If they meant for each other as soul mates, then it will become a very sad fate for this pair. But I will show you how to make their relationship worked later. To make it easy, I have created a simple diagram for easy understanding (see Figure 2).

When a person falls into the lower level of your connection, you will also see lesser details of each other profile. Because of that, sometimes people don't connect with 3rd level or lower as they assumed that profile is either fake or not an active user.

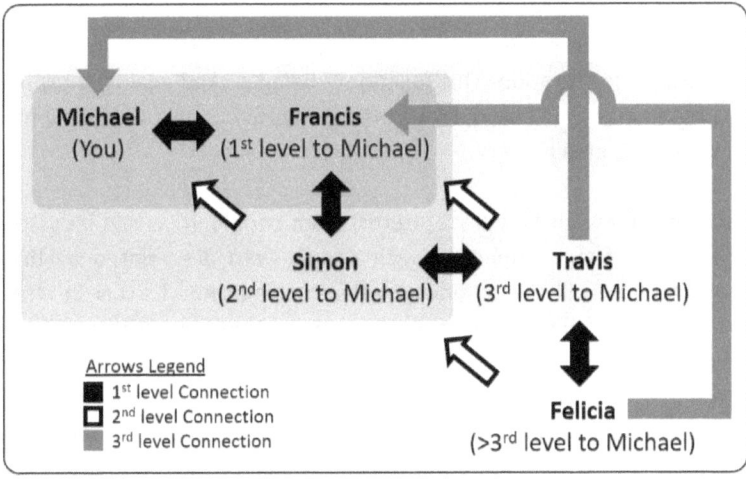

Figure 2: LinkedIn's various levels of connection

As you can see, the more 1st level connections you have, you will get more notice and reach from the 2nd level connections. If you reach out to more 3rd level connections and get connected with them to become your 1st level connections, guess what? You now get more down lines of 2nd and 3rd level connections. Got the idea?

So if you want to crack this algorithm, the answer is simple: - find people to connect with. When you think harder, you will realise you don't just want to connect with people, you want to connect with people with a lot of 1st level connections of their own so that their 1st level becomes your 2nd level! However, you will come to realise, after linking up with your family, friends, colleagues and maybe even your neighbours, you probably run out of people to connect. Adding to that, some of them only have you as connection, you are not getting 2nd level from them. This is not going to work!

Relax my friend, in the LinkedIn community, there are two acronyms to help you with that. Those who indicate "L.I.O.N" and "No IDK" under their profiles are worth connecting. L.I.O.N means "LinkedIn Open Networker" and No IDK means "No I don't know". The former is self-explanatory that means the profile welcomes linking up. While the latter means if for some reasons, I don't want to connect with you, I will not click the popup question "I don't know you" function after I rejected your invitation. This function if being clicked against a profile too many times, will block him from inviting to connect unless he has that profile's email.

Let's say you want to attract interest from people in certain industry. Then apart from connecting with people who are related to that industry, you will try to find people that indicates L.I.O.N in their profiles. But some people might say, "But I don't know this people, why should I connect with them?" Just like in Facebook and any other social media platform, if you want to increase your reach and network, you can't just rely on your family and friends to sell your products and services. If you want someone to refer or offer you a job, good luck staying connected only with your colleagues. They probably want the job as much as you. You need to connect with the hiring managers, the human resource personnel and the head-hunters. You can't just connect with all of them, but you might connect with a L.I.O.N profile with 1,000 connections of such who can potentially become your 2nd level.

Now that you understand this connection concept, don't just go around connecting with L.I.O.N profiles. There is a downside in this and you need to have a balance. L.I.O.N profiles although they have many connections, not all of them are active in supporting other posts. As mentioned, LinkedIn members tend to care about their own affairs more than anything else and even though they are connected to you, some are only interested to gain your 2nd level connections and vice versa. Hence, you have to look at their activity history and see if they are active in taking interest of others. Some L.I.O.N profiles like the idea of big network for self-gain but they are typically not interested in others without meeting their own agenda first.

Another type of profile that is worth connecting are those with high number of followers. Such profile tends to be a proven record of adding value to the LinkedIn community and have attracted a good number of followers. They are likely to be very active and engaging. A way to find out is to look for a profile with at least 10,000 followers and look at his activity history again. If you see he has been contributing a lot of positive comments to people's posts, then he is a worthy connection.

One thing to highlight. Regardless whether the profile is a L.I.O.N or not, always personalised your invitation. Don't just ask to connect without giving a reason. You can say things like, "I found you under my recommended connections", "I believe in the power of networking", "We have some mutual connections", "We shared similar industry / interest", "I like your post in that post", etc. Plenty of reasons to connect, just think of something and be sincere with your invitation. That way, people don't see you as a scam or just want another connection for no purpose.

Now here is a question for you, after finding a lot of likeminded people, connecting with them and engaging with them for a while, what's next? My advice is don't stop there. Go back to the traditional way of networking. Take the relationship to the next level. Turn the connection to a potential friendship. Ask them out for a drink. I say a drink, not a meal. Do you know why? Well, like any blind date, if you don't feel comfortable with the meet up, you can just finish up that ristretto and give an excuse to move on for the next appointment without any awkwardness. But if you ordered a 3-course meal, you may be stuck with at least an hour of unpleasant conversation and risk impairing that new relationship. Not all meet ups will turn up into deepen friendships but never burn your bridges.

2. Common Interests

In the past, the LinkedIn algorithms do not emphasis on this as much. But with the trend of the sorting system, LinkedIn has made progression in the measurement of common interest. This is partly to deal with spams and fake accounts. Mainly, it is to prevent too much non-related content feeding members' newsfeed. Because of that, LinkedIn algorithm identifies members' personal backgrounds, interest groups, hashtags and pages they follow. Adding to that, it also takes into account the similar interest in content sharing, engagement language and the associated industries.

What is the impact of this algorithm? It controls where the content will flow within your network. For example, if you are sharing an Oil & Gas related topic, the content will prioritise the content to go into the newsfeed of Oil & Gas professionals. It doesn't mean it will not flow into non-Oil & Gas professionals but to a lesser extent. However, if a non-Oil & Gas professional has been continually engaging in those type of posts related to that author, it will prioritise that into his newsfeed as well.

You probably have a good idea on how to crack this algorithm to work for you. Nevertheless, allow me to share my humble experience on this. There are three approaches to this:

a. Request to join related groups to your interest
b. Find and use specific hashtags with big followers
c. Use specific keywords in your profile and content

a. Request to join related groups to your interest

Like Facebook interest group, you will be using the same strategies but slightly modified and lesser steps.

Step 1 – Request to join a related interest group. Find groups with more than 50,000 members if possible. LinkedIn allow you to join up to 100 groups.

Step 2 – Engage in the activities of those groups.

Step 3 – Do step 2 for at least 2 weeks to get yourself noticed.

Step 4 – Post your content as per normal and then share further in the groups. The reason for sharing instead of posting the original in groups is to allow easy tracking back to your original post and linked it to your profile. Engage further, but don't neglect step 2.

Step 5 – Invite the current members to follow your personal hashtags (will explain that later).

One thing to note. Don't share your posts excessively in those groups. Once or twice a week in a group is fine. You don't want to appear spamming the specific group and turn the members off. Also, some groups need the admins to approve your content before it will be listed in the group.

Eventually when you gain more followers from those groups, you can move away from there. This is by creating specific hashtags in your content and asking the members to follow if they want to continue receiving them.

b. Find and use specific hashtags with big followers

This is an easy approach, google the top hashtags in LinkedIn and put the related one under your posts. This will reflect on people's newsfeed on the hashtags they are following. However, don't go all crazy listing as many hashtags as possible. I had come across that and they look like desperate posts seeking attention. 1 or 2 hashtags is enough, be specific, be professional.

c. Use specific keywords in your profile and content

The last one is easy as well, include as many keywords related to how you want to brand yourself in your profile and content.

For example, if you are an accountant, your keywords will be tax, audit, bookkeeping, payroll, costing, etc. The more you reflect these key words into your profile and experience, the higher chance people will find you and your content. For example, if a recruiter is looking for an accountant, it will not search by your name. Instead, it will search by the role name and a few associated key words. Again, do some research and find out the most hit rate of keywords people use. There are many websites that provide such information. It makes sense isn't it? If you want people to hunt you for what you are worth and talented for, don't you want to highlight those keywords as much as possible?

3. Engagement Rate

In the past, LinkedIn engagement algorithms are not very difficult to crack. As long you get many likes, the post can go viral. Because of that, the LinkedIn newsfeed have been flooded with nuisance and non-value-added posts and people wondered how the heck did people support such posts when informative posts didn't even get a single reaction. Even a one-two liner posts can get people going crazy. This is not good for LinkedIn business when the platform becomes poor in professional marketing and people start to become less active in engagement.

As such, LinkedIn has been progressively improved the engagement algorithms. Before we go into details, let's look at some engagement terms. The engagement rate is typically made up of the following measurable factors:

  i. Clicks
 ii. Shares
iii. Likes
 iv. Comments
  v. New followers
 vi. Revisit impressions
vii. Dwell time

The total engagement is the sum of all the above. Before mid-2019, as long there are many clicks, likes or any of the factors, the engagement score can go very high. Some websites offered such service at a decent price to go to your content to like and give basic comments. However, such posts don't actually represent the real engagement. Hence, the scoring system has changed to put different weight on the factors. The most impactful factor is the comments. Apart from dropping plain unconstructive comments, the LinkedIn measures if a comment is constructive and whether it warrants a response. If more people start replying not just only to the post but to the comments related, behaving like a group discussion, the engagement scores will rise more significantly.

When engagement efforts increase, the revisit impressions and dwell time will also increase in scoring as participants will revisit that post and dwell longer to respond.

The way to beat this system is to have contents that are not just informative but encourage participation. Stir them to ask questions or provide answers. When people leave comments, encourage further response by seeking clarification or more insights. But here is the tricky thing, with the excessive posts flooding the newsfeeds, what are the odds to get the engagement scores high? This brings to the next factor: - the "Golden Hour". Everyone repeats this after me, "Woooaaahhhhh…, golden hour!!!"

4. Golden Hour

This is probably the most important algorithm. Without this, the rest of the factors will not take precedence. It is called the golden hour because all the engagement factors play a more significant role in the first hour. This algorithm is also the reason why LinkedIn posts have poorer traffic compared to Facebook. Partly because most LinkedIn posts are public instead of private (for only connections or group selective views). The engagement rate is critical during the golden hour. If you don't meet the golden hour performance, the remaining hours will not have much impact. I will elaborate further on the view rate algorithm next but for the start, it is number of views on your post. The below table is a tested data to give you a good guide.

Number of views within the golden hour	Potential final number of views after life cycle	Life cycle
300 to 1000	2K to 10K	Up to a day
1001 to 1200	10K to 30K	Up to 2 days
1201 to 1500	30K to 75K	Up to 4 days
1501 to 1800	75K to 150K	Up to a week
>1801	Are you kidding me?!	Up to 2 weeks

Figure 3: View rate guide for golden hour

Basically, in a nutshell, if you hit 1,000 views on your post within the golden hour, the potential number of views will go up to 10,000 counts by different people. It doesn't count the views of the same person (that is parked under revisit impressions factor). After the life cycle is determined, it doesn't mean the post will stop getting views but it will drop significantly and flush down the pecking order in the news feed. Hence, the first hour of engagement is critical. Now you can see why there are websites selling followers to support your posts as a business? Again, I will strongly discourage that if you want organic growth in your branding. Just like content and reach, quality and quantity are equally important in your followers for branding.

There are 3 ways to crack this golden hour system.

The 1st way is tagging people under the comments whom you think will enjoy the post. Within 2 minutes, this will send an immediate notification to them that they are being mentioned. After the 2 minutes mark, even when you removed the tags, their notifications remain intact.

The 2nd approach is creating a LinkedIn group chat under messaging and send the link of the post and ask for support from your regular connections. This approach can only use sparingly as you don't want to annoy your connections regularly. Also, depends on how active your connections are, the first and second approach may not meet the golden hour requirement.

Hence, the 3rd method is my preferred way which has been the most effective. Look for around 10 to 25 connections who are also interested to build their branding. Form a messaging group using WhatsApp or WeChat to align everyone on the golden hour requirement. Everyone will post around the same time, request and provide the engagement supports. Personally, you don't want to have a group bigger than 25 as it will be excessive work managing all the requests. Additionally, you want to build the group relationship further and it is easier with a smaller group.

5. Timing of Post

The timing is not actually an algorithm factor on its own but it plays a major part in triggering the rest of the algorithms effectively. The problem about this factor is if you read online, there will be all kind of recommendations and you will end up trial and error extensively. So here is an honest guide for you.

The timing you choose to publish your post depends on the geographic dynamic of your connections. If majority of your connections are in Singapore, then stick to the Singapore time zone. You don't want to post in the middle of the night and hope for good engagement during the golden hour. That is the first rule. The next step is to understand the hot timings.

Typically, statistics have proven that majority of the people check on their LinkedIn accounts when they are: -

1) commuting to work,
2) during their tea breaks in office,
3) during lunch breaks, and
4) travel home and before dinner.

1, 3 and 4 are longer timing while 2 is short. In Singapore context, people typically travel to work between 8am to 9am and travel home after 5pm. Lunch is generally between 12pm to 2pm. And recruiters tend to be known for being active around 10am after their morning meetings (useful if you want them to seek you for job opportunities).

Over the years, I have also tested out on different contents in relation to the timing and I found that light hearted posts tend to attract a lot of attention during lunch breaks and after 5pm (end of the day work). If you are very specific in targeting a company's attention with your content, it is worth doing a bit of due diligence to find out their working hours.

One key point to highlight, don't post excessively. Quality is more important than quantity. I will recommend 1 to 2 posts a day. Don't flood your connections' newsfeed until they choose to unfollow or block you. Once they do that, it will end up like the Facebook personal account, people typically don't follow you back.

6. View Rate Data and Social Selling Index (SSI)

I find the view rate data a very useful guide to see how well your content has performed. Once you have done on the cracking of algorithms above, the view rate data is like a report card of your performance. I will be using Figure 4 as an example of my video post on the assembly of Airbus A380. My intention is to get attention of people from the aviation industry.

On the left column, it shows the industry of the people who viewed my video. As you can see, I have managed to capture all the aviation people's attention. In the middle column, it narrows down on the background of job title of these people. Typically, I will disregard the top list with Salesperson title. The reason for that is many LinkedIn users still haven't changed their job title under their profiles and it is defaulted as salesperson. Based on my post, I have managed to capture CEOs / Executive Directors as my top list. Have you wondered how many CEOs / Executive Directors caught an attention of you in your whole career? A video post like this did the job in a day. On the right column, it shows the geographic dynamics of the people. This gives you an idea how well timed is your post. Also, it provides the information of whether this post captured the right interest group. For this post, you will see many French taking interest, which proves that the Airbus is relevant to them, since the company is based in France.

If the data doesn't reflect the type of people you want to capture the attention, then you need to go back to the above factors and improve further.

The other good report card of your profile is the Social Selling Index. I have found this much better than the Facebook's insights because it categorised the areas on where I did well and where I can improve. You can find your SSI with this link www.linkedin.com/sales/ssi.

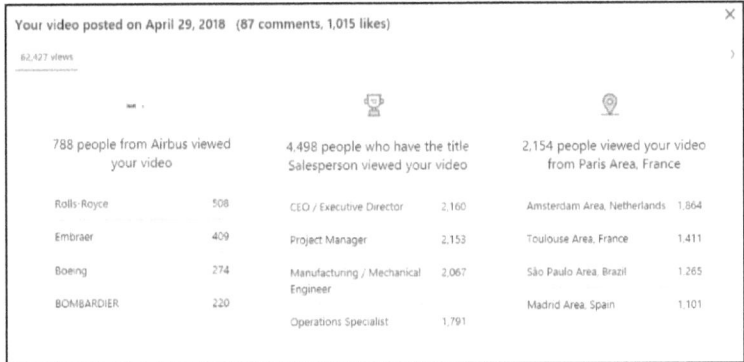

Figure 4: Content view rate data

Figure 5: Social Selling Index example

The SSI is divided into 4 categories (see Figure 5), namely:

a. Establish your professional brand
b. Find the right people
c. Engage with insights
d. Build relationships

From the four categories, it will calculate where you stand in your social branding within the industry you are in and within your network. Looking at Figure 6, you will see I am ranked at top 1% among the Management Consulting Industry and also among my network.

Why is this useful? Let's say someone did a search for a Management Consultant, I will always position in the 1st page of the search results. The chances of that someone checking me out is very likely. Typically, people hardly go beyond 3rd page of the search results. So, if you want a recruiter to find you through search for an opportunity in a specific industry, you need to be well positioned in their radar.

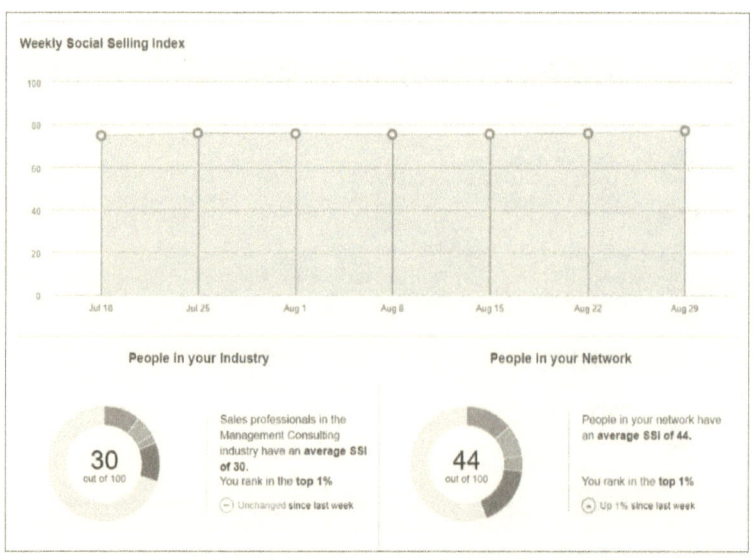

Figure 6: Social Selling Index industry and network rankings

The next thing I am going to share is how to improve these scoring.

a. Establish your professional brand

The basic portion of this is to tidy up your profile to be as comprehensive as possible. The more people click on your profile and dwell on it, the higher the scoring. One of the best approaches is writing articles. When people check on your profile and spend time reading your articles, that scoring is going to improve significant.

b. Find the right people

This scoring is not easy to maintain. Basically, it is finding specific people through industry or title using the LinkedIn search function, then invite to connect. Checking out other people's profiles through the search helps as well but not significant score rate. There are only so many people you can connect and eventually it will stabilise.

c. Engage with insights

This relates to how well you contribute in the LinkedIn community. Sharing LinkedIn recommended posts, commenting on others' contents and replying to your own posts' comments. Wordy comments tend to do the job well.

d. Build relationships

This is the easiest scoring factor compared to the rest. LinkedIn will always notify you on your connections' birthdays, work anniversaries, etc. Click on those connections to congratulate them. Do that regularly and it will hit full score. This is always a good opportunity to catch up with your network and also filter out non-active connections.

7. Social Sharing

I find social sharing useful at times. This is not an algorithm itself but a good approach to get attention. How does it work?
Let's say you want to get into the radar of a high-profile person that you are not connected to. Sending him an invite may not work as he might be selective in the people he wants to connect. Also, he has not seen any values in connecting with you. Hence, what you can do is to look into his activities and see what are the posts or comments he has done. If there is a post that might be interest to you, give an insightful comment under his post and then share that post, tagging him and give further insights. Subsequently, see if he responds to you. If not, send him a personal message to thank him for the particular post and

provide further insightful comments. If he responded, offer to connect and see if you can take that relationship further.

Ok, how's that for professional social media algorithms? If you follow the steps well, you will build your brand in no time. But now the burning question is how to make it sustainable? You will find cracking the algorithms are much easier than writing contents. And how to do it for years?

Don't worry. I am not going to leave you hanging like that. In my own case, I have been doing for more than 3 years, posting almost every day with quality contents. I was able to derive a model that helps to build contents. This is what this book is about and I am going to share that with you next in the following chapter.

10. Cross-Linked Individual Branding Model (CLIB)

Cross-Linked Individual Branding Model (CLIB)

Here comes the most exciting part of this book. What I am about to share with you is something I created, tested and perfected over the last few years. It is not just going to give you success in content writing, but also going to build your brand with long sustaining results. Yes, long sustaining is what I aim to help you achieve. Why is that important? Let me share with you how it all started.

In the past, I wanted to learn more about content writing and went on a searching spree for a content writing guru. I didn't find any, at least not by my standards. Maybe my expectations are too high or I just have no luck finding the right one. Every time I come across a profile that said he is a trainer in content writing, the next thing I did is to check the type of contents he has written and how regular he has posted his contents. There are always three things lacking: - 1) the contents are not as impressive as I expect from a content writing coach, 2) he doesn't post regularly which I am expecting from someone who claim to create content with ease, and 3) there are not many reactions on those posts.

Because of that, I can't bring myself to pay for that kind of standards. Having said that, I am not discrediting content writer trainers here. They do share some useful tips. The key takeaways I get from them is to write what really matters to oneself and topics that people can benefit from. However, being a systematic person, I still want to find out the structure to give me the ability to produce contents regularly on a long-term basis. How can I achieve that? I did a research on people who posted contents regularly and classify them into 2 groups. The first group will just post anything that comes to their mind or sharing videos that they probably come across from somewhere that can help them get a lot of reactions. Their writings are typically short without much value but with the intent to gain attention by posing questions to get responses. The second group does share quality contents but I realised they write about themselves most of the time. Majority of them keep repeating their stories and there is only that much values you can benefit from their stories. Don't get me wrong, there are many ways to write and promote about ourselves; that is the whole idea of achieving personal branding. But there is a fine line of direct self-promoting versa values promoting. One promotes self to gain popularity, while the other promotes values through self to gain popularity. At that point, I am still at square one trying to find a structure that can achieve the latter. Though from those who posted regularly, the key thing I have learned is that you can write more contents when you talked about your own interests or experiences. Point taken on that.

The next thing I decided to do is search for branding gurus. I came across some really good brand strategists that provide the whole thought process of creating a brand. The concept is very good in regards of what values a brand should bring and who are the target audiences. However, the downside is there is no clear formulas nor models to achieve that in terms of content writing.

Being confused myself, I decided to make out my own purposes. After giving some long thoughts, I came up with three generic points: -

1. Create attention and awareness
2. Drawn likeminded people to me
3. Be seen as an "expert" in the subject matter

How did I come about deriving them? Why didn't I include a point like "make others like me?". The main reason is I want the roots of the purpose to achieve the fruits. Making people to like me is one of the fruits but I can't control it; I can't make everyone like me. And in order to achieve that, I need likeminded people's attention. Once they notice me and like me, there is an opportunity to cultivate that further. When I was thinking about this deeper, it also takes me into a journey of self-discovery. I thought about what kind of job I want, what kind of work environment I want to be in, and most importantly, I want people to appreciate for who I am and what I am capable of. I always wondered why some people can change jobs smoothly through their networks and climb up their career ladder effectively. Then I looked back at some of my previous jobs and the interviews I have.

In those interviews that went very smoothly into job offers, I realised the interviewers didn't judge me on my capabilities. They don't doubt me on that. The main thing they assessed me for is whether I can fit into their organisation culture, do I have the character and personality that align with their existing employees. Adding to that, the interviewers are usually the people whom have already either known me in some ways or heard from someone who speaks good things about me. In that extent, it has already given them a certain level of confidence to hire me.

I believe in many cases in the corporate world, people tend to hire someone whom they are familiar and will enjoy working with. Put it this way, let's say there is a senior role available in your company and you are asked to give possible recommendations. You thought of two persons you have worked with in the past. The first person is highly competent to fit the role but you don't always see things eye-to-eye with him. In fact, you and him have some differences that doesn't help in the relationship. The second person is probably 70% competent to suit the role but he is a great person to work with. You have high regards for his principles and ethics plus you really like his character. Who are you likely to recommend? I rest my case, character and personality is more favoured compared to competencies.

You can keep talking about how capable you are but if no one vouch for your character, you are not going to get much recommendations or referrals. Of course, I am not saying you can just ignore promoting your competencies. But it has to come with the right character in applying the skills. Therefore, in order to achieve being seen as an "expert" in the subject matter, I have learned how to present myself with my character as the front and articulate my content from that angle. Instead of saying I did this and that, I have to think about how I went about achieving them. How did I approach those tasks and why did I did it that way?

That took my journey of self-discovery even further. I realised the way I undertake my tasks and how I live my personal life have many similarities to how I work in the corporate world and vice versa. For example, being a true-blue engineer (as I self-proclaimed), I like the challenge of problem solving. Because of that, in all my jobs, I am renowned by my peers to be very good in that aspect. Many of my career achievements are derived from that as well. Interestingly, that characteristic also relates to why I enjoyed solving puzzles, fixing stuff at home and even doing art & craft. There is a definite relation of who I am and what I do in life, at work and in personal life. With this revelation, I believe I can build some contents for my personal branding.

For example, instead of telling people of my problem-solving skills and appearing to them as if I am trying to promote my ego, I shared about my interest in solving puzzles. From that angle, I can rouse the attention of likeminded people who are into puzzles. Let me show you an example.

Content title: Puzzle Fix

"Do you like to play jigsaw puzzles? I love it. My favourites are those thousand-pieces sets in famous arts.

The trick of completing a puzzle has some similarities in managing a business, which can be summed up in 3 points.

1) First, find the flat pieces to form the border. Like a business, before you can construct the whole picture, create an outline. It will be the foundation to build your structure.

2) Grouping your pieces in terms of colour, by comparing it to the original picture. In business, even though every functional group serves different purposes, they must always reflect back to the original plan. Gathering your resources and build them up strategically. If you randomly just picked a piece to fill the puzzle, you will never get it right.

3) Separate the unknown pieces that can't fit into any groups. Identify them and wait for the opportunity to fit them into the puzzle. In every business, never discard creativity. There will always be something unique that may not fit in at a certain point. But always keep a lookout as that missing piece might be the final piece.

To run any business, you need to see it as a 10,000 pieces puzzle instead of 100 pieces. The bigger it is, the more effective you will look into strategic planning.

"Life isn't about finding pieces of a puzzle, it's about putting those exceptional pieces together." - Glenn van Dekken"

How do you find the example above? By telling them how I solved puzzles, it drawn attention from people who are familiar about puzzles. When I talked about the approach I used, I am adding values for them to learn to appreciate my problem-solving approach. If I can articulate that effectively, people will likely cultivate their own perspectives and believe that I am good in problem solving. They can gain some insights and knowledge from my sharing. While I am able to keep promoting my contents along that line, eventually people will start to believe I am an "expert" in problem solving. This is like a Eureka moment for me. I went straight to the drawing board and mock-up the following diagram (see Figure 7). On the left side which I parked my professional life, I categorised it into previous work experiences, current role and future desired role / experiences I wished to achieve. On the right side, I created my personal life and categorised it into my hobbies (things I do to relax), lifestyles (my current and desired lifestyles) and passions (what are the things I am inspired and passionate about).

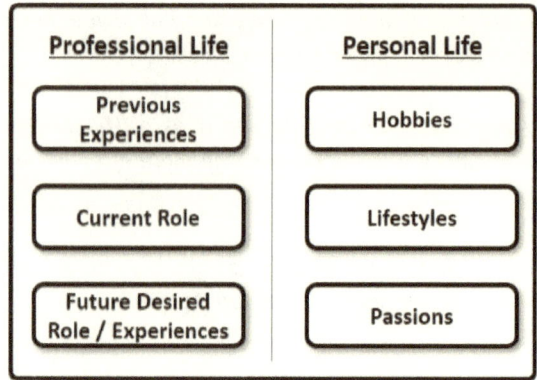

Figure 7: Initial mock-up of Cross-Linked Individual Branding (CLIB) model

In the next step, I try to fill up these categories as much as possible. For the reason of personal privacy, I will use of one of my students' example. For training purposes, I have also simplified it as the original is actually much more comprehensive, see Figure 8.

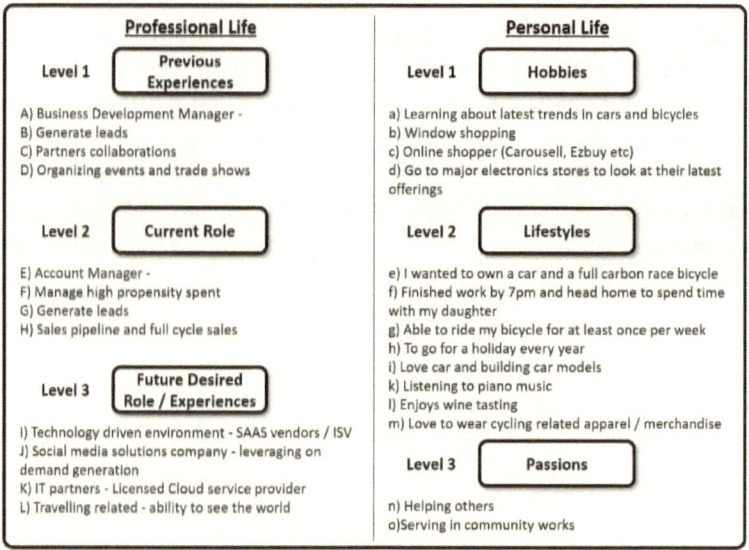

Figure 8: 2nd step CLIB model – Filled up the categories

In all the items on the left, I will assign the big capital letters to identified them individually and likewise, small capital letters for the right. Also, I have given levels to each category, the higher the level, the more weight it carries. There are reasons for all these but before we get into that, the 3rd step is to highlight the key words in those items. See Figure 9 for the texts in bold and underlined as key words.

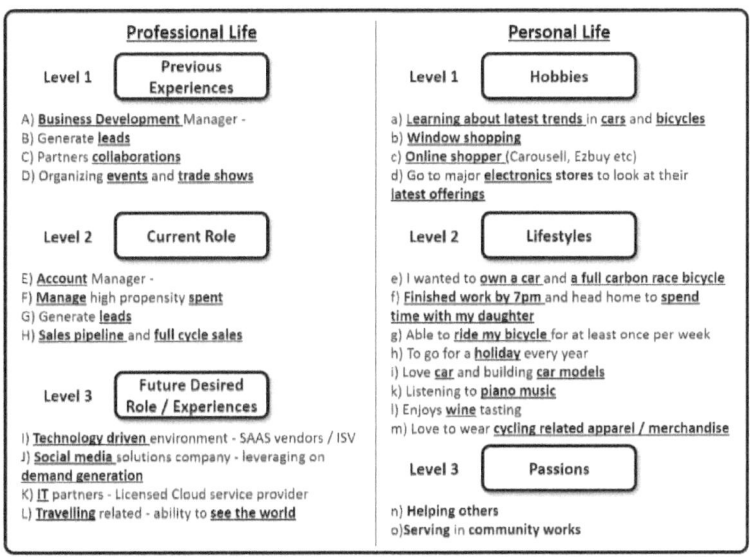

Figure 9: 3rd step CLIB model – Highlight the key words

After the 3rd step, you can easily have an idea what this person is like. In a quick snapshot, you can tell he is an outgoing person based on his Sales role and cycling hobbies. He is into online shopping and social media, keeping up with trends, enjoys travelling, appreciate instrumental music like piano and wine tasting, putting him into a more like a "hunter" sales guy than a "farming" sales guy. His passion in helping others also put him in a position likely to be a sincere sales person that aims to solve customers' problems. Can you see how much correlation in this person's professional and personal life? This overall also gives a snapshot to tell if the person is really happy in his current job and whether he has what it takes to achieve his desired career role.

I strongly believed the kind of career journey that we take has a lot of things in common on how we live our lives. We are what we do because of certain character and personality traits. For example, if you simply looked at the right side of the profile given, you will see little traits if he wants to be an accountant or financial related roles. Based on the fact that there are little indications in conventional or enterprising interests such as investing, hobbies related to data analysis, detailed stuff like interior design, risk taking and decision making.

Interesting so far? Wait, it is getting more exciting!

The 4th step is the fun part and you will realise why. It is an endless process of self-discovery. Like the example I given above on profiling the person, I will compare all the items on the left and right further and identify anything in common. For example, his interest in generating leads as a sales person (professional life: B & G) can have some similarity in his interest in online shopping (personal life: b & c); they both seem to be about exploring opportunities, looking for good deals and observing the market trends. From there, I will cross-link the left and right items and make a note on why they are linked. As it is going to get pretty messy, therefore, you can now appreciate why I assigned the big and small capital alphabetic arrangement. Figure 10 gives you a good idea after all the connections.

Some people might ask, "What if I can't find a lot of similarity?" That has been proven as well. If your professional and personal life is very dissimilar, there is a high tendency that you are not really enjoying your work. For example, imagine a person who is currently working as musician but he wanted a quiet lifestyle without disturbance. Kind of mismatch in career isn't it? Who can earn a living by playing music but doesn't want to be seen by others, let alone being heard? But if the person still really wants to pursue a music career, then he may want to reconsider adjusting his personal lifestyle. Again, it is about self-discovery.

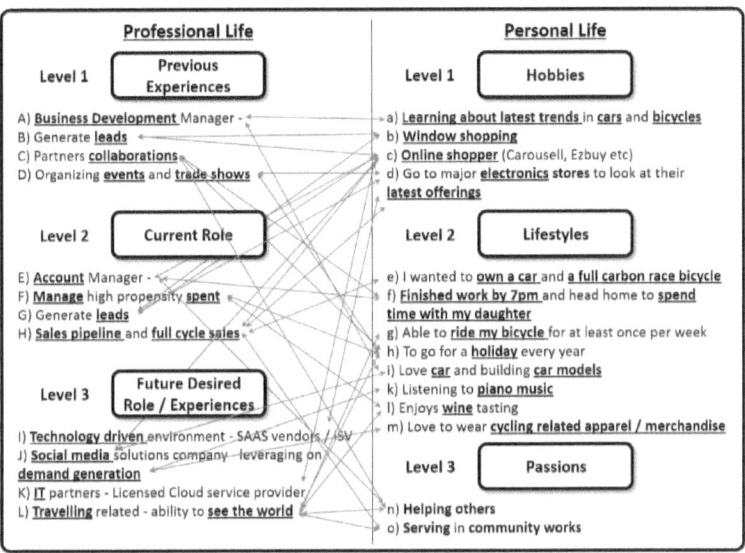

Figure 10: 4th step CLIB model – Cross-link the left and right items

To make things easier to understand from Figure 10, I have also created a table to list out all the cross-linked items (see Figure 11). The 5th step is the associated level to get a score. Example, for cross-linked item "Jm", "J" is at professional life level 3 while "m" is at personal life level 2. Therefore, the multiplication score is 6. The score implications are put into 3 categories, score 1 to 3, 4 to 6 and 9. Score 1 to 3 is what I termed a "Seeker", cross-linked items in this area represent things typical of people's comfort zone or early career experience. Typically, there tend to be more items falling into this category. Score 4 to 6 is what I called an "Explorer". Cross-linked items in this area shows an experienced explorer, looking for new paths and adventures while at the same time, have a good idea what he is seeking. Score 9 is where you are in your prime, living a dream job and dream life. In this example, there is only two cross-linked items "Ln" and "Lo". There is a likelihood this person will enjoy a fulfilling job if he can travel around the world and helping others in the community.

Cross-Linked Items	Professional Level × Personal Level Score	Score Implications	
Aa, Bb, Bc, Dd	1	• Comfortable zone • Doing what you are always been doing but not necessary satisfying • Money may be the priority	Seeker
Ai, Cf, Ch, Dh, Eb, Gb, Gc, Gd, He, Hd, Id, Jc	2		
Cn, Kc	3		
Ef, Fh, Fl, He	4	• Leaning to lifestyle and possibly work life balance • Doing what you are likely to enjoy • You are happy with what you are doing	Explorer
Eo, Ho, Jk, Jm, Lg, Lh, Ll	6		
Ln, Lo	9	• Dream career • Something you are pursuing or enjoy doing for a long run • Things you strongly believe and reflects your character	Prime

Figure 11: Cross-linked items, associated scoring and scoring implications

At this stage, once you have cross-linked all the items, you have successfully individualised everything about yourself in terms of your professional and personal life. The final step is looking at all the items and build content around it. This is the most important part because your personal branding is determined by this. You will also realise the contents associated cross-linked items with higher scores have more impact to achieve stronger personal branding and creating in-roads for your future desired career opportunities. To help you establish better understanding, let's look at a few examples.

Cross-linked example 1
"Gd" – "Generate leads" vs "Go to major electronics stores to look at their latest offerings".

The key similarity of these two items is the person's ability to search for opportunities and good deals. This is a talent in its own way. A few contents that can be created related to this is how he goes about searching for good deals in electronics, how he compared the key advantages and disadvantages before deciding ranking them in potentials. He can relate this on how he applies the same principle when it comes to generating sale leads. The following is the content example.

"Are you into gadgets? I am an avid collector of gadgets and enjoyed exploring new gadgets and study how it can really help my daily needs. It is probably a man's thing and his toys. However, it is not a cheap hobby to maintain. Hence, I will always explore the market and find out more about the product's specifications, prices and whether it is worth buying. One of the methods I do is going to major electronics stores and striking conversations with the sales representatives. From there, you can gain a lot of insights from them on the product's trends in terms for value and prices.

Similarly, when it comes to my sales role in generating leads, part of my approach is making conversations with people. It sounds simple though in order to encourage people to engage with you, you must first let them feel your sincerity and cultivate their trust in you. Only then can they open up more and share their valuable knowledge."

Does the above appeal to you? Firstly, when things like "gadgets" and "shopping around" are mentioned, many people with the same interest can relate to it. The approach is nothing new but when he related it to how he does his sales job, people can appreciate his way of doing things. By pointing out some suggestions like "feel your sincerity" and "cultivating their trust", he is adding values through sharing his own experience. Don't you think readers can respect him as a sales professional?

Cross-linked example 2
"Fh" – "Manage high propensity spent" vs "To go for a holiday every year".

The key similarity of these two items is budget management and planning. We all know that when it comes to holidays, two factors that are always considered are the length of the stay and how much budget available. Only from there, can the holiday be well planned. In a sales role, managing and measuring clients' potential is also a skillset. Can you see how many contents can derive from this angle? How we spent on holidays and managing clients' unforeseen spending behaviour can also be another talking point. Overspending in holidays and controlling clients' spending is also another topic. How about a bad holiday? How do you spend in such situation? Perhaps a similar experience with a client who loses interest in supporting your sales? How do you work around it?

You can relate so much from both experiences. The best part of this is many people can relate themselves to holidays and the contents can definitely catch their attention.

Cross-linked example 3
"Eo" – "Account Manager" vs "Serving in community works".

What does these two have in commons? There are quite a few if you look deeper. To function in both roles well, the person will have to enjoy communicating with people, listening to them, finding ways to serve their needs, spending time building relationships, just to name a few. In all these attributes, there are plenty of life experience and stories to tell. If you keep talking along this line, don't you think people will perceive you as a caring person who looks into other people's interest? If an organisation wanted an Account Manager who not just help them to make money but most importantly, holding such values to ensure long term relationships with their clients, don't you want them to notice you for that?

Here you go, we have finally covered everything about the CLIB model. To summarise, the following are the 7 steps:

Step 1: Prepared your own preferred writing materials, be in pen / paper or excel spreadsheet. On the left side, list your professional life's categories of A) previous work experiences, B) current role and C) future desired role / experiences. On the right side, created your personal life's categories of a) hobbies, b) lifestyles & c) passions.

Step 2: Fill up these categories with related items as much as possible.

Step 3: Highlight all the keywords in the items.

Step 4: Compare the items between the professional life vs personal life.

Step 5: Cross-link the items.

Step 6: List out the cross-linked items onto a table and calculate the scores.

Step 7: Looked into cross-linked items and build the contents.

There are three typical questions my students will ask and I will like to address them here as well. The first question is in regards to the amount of time that will take to complete the model. So far, most of my students take less than a day. But honestly, it really depends how much effort you put your thoughts into it. The more comprehensive it is created, the more relevant your branding content will become. I will also encourage you to revisit the CLIB model you have created periodically because we will mature over time and our priorities, needs and wants may also change with that as well.

The second question is if I am running my side-line business as well as working full-time, do I market myself in the same model? The simple answer is no. It is better to keep your contents separate if you are doing another side line that might conflict in your personal branding. If that side-line business for some reasons, didn't turn up well, it will not affect your career personal branding. Having said that, I will touch on the CLIB for business / entrepreneur applications next. The third question my students always ask if why don't I give more examples? The answer is straightforward, you need to develop your own personal branding using the model and not the examples. If not, the CLIB model will have failed its concept.

11. CLIB for Business & Entrepreneur Applications

CLIB for Business & Entrepreneur Applications

When I started using the CLIB model for my personal branding in LinkedIn, I also did some testing on Facebook. Together with the understanding in cracking the algorithms, results came fast. As such I begin to share the model with some of my peers and see if it works for them, with the understanding that it is only meant for their personal use and not for circulation. Everyone came out with great results and those who are consistent in applying them have also achieved and maintained good personal branding of their owns. Words of mouth soon came and I have people reaching out for some advices on personal branding. I did share with a few acquaintances some insights, but not comprehensively. However, a few events happened thereafter which stopped me from doing so. After sharing a few tricks, some people took that little knowledge and decide to become coaches on branding in LinkedIn. Somehow my integrity doesn't allow that. It is not about trying to earn a living as a coach but it is about honesty. That little knowledge is not enough to help others in their branding and may even have adverse results. They became coaches is to help themselves more than helping others. My deepest concern came to realisation when a few of my networks shared their bad experiences from these coaches and I felt partly responsible. From then on, I decided if I really want to help, do it as a consultative work. I choose not to share out of kindness without thinking of the consequences. That is how it leads me to apply the CLIB model for business people.

Because of what happened and by accident, my services became known and I was approached by a few small business owners for consultation in improving the branding of their businesses. I spent a lot of time listening to them and understanding their business challenges. In most cases, I realised the key challenge they faced is the alignment between them and their customers. That lack of understanding between them often leads to conflicts, bad decisions and even losses. From there, I recognised a lot of issues due to alignment challenges can be resolved by the CLIB model. However, I have to modify the model a little to cater for business application. Hence, the left-hand side was changed from professional life to entrepreneur life (See Figure 12).

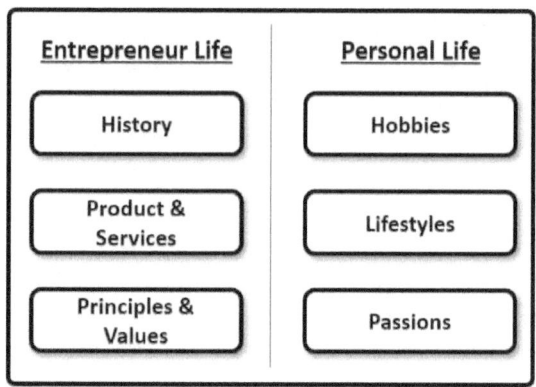

Figure 12: Initial mock-up of Cross-Linked Individual Branding (CLIB) model

The approach is the same but the categories have to revolve around the business. For the first category, I choose history as it is something that I felt is of great importance. I believe every entrepreneur starts their business with a great belief in something. Whether is a market new niche or an opportunity to fulfil people's needs, they are very certain why the business concept will work. That's why they took the leap of faith to become an entrepreneur. How it all begins matter. The sad part for some entrepreneurs is that after some time, they themselves forgot how it all started. Along the way when they are pressurised by market expectations and demands, they deviate from what they wanted to do for their business, keeping the customers and everyone else happy except themselves. They became miserable being entrepreneurs and find no joy in it. They lost their grounds. Hence, remember the history: how it all starts, how it develops, the challenges and breakthroughs that set the business foundation is an integral part of the business branding. The best part is when this is written well, it will just get better as the business gets older. People appreciates businesses with good histories.

The second category is without doubt the business' products and services. It is the pride of the business success. The problem that a lot of businesses face is that they may emphasis too much on promoting the image of their products and services but not the values of them. They focus on the packaging and outlooks but not the tangible results. If you want to sell oranges, don't talk about how orange the oranges are, talk about the amount of vitamin C it can bring to a good health. That brings to the third and last category, principles and values. Without this, a business holds no ground and will be at the mercy of everyone. Instead of allowing others pushing their demands across, they must be made aware the principles and values of the business. That is not made during business negotiations or during customer engagements. It must be imprinted in their mindset before they stepped into the business' premises. And only through branding can that be articulate clearly.

Just like the previous setup, the next step is to fill up these categories as much as possible and highlight the keywords. I will be using one of my client's example in simplified format for training purposes (see Figure 13). In the next step, we do our usual CSI profiling investigation of all the identified evidences.

In a snapshot of the example, you can tell the person enjoys study fashion trends and manage to apply that in her business. She enjoys colouring which probably shows her good sense in fashion. Her interests in baking, gardening, long walks and travelling to countryside places showed that she enjoys nature and practical stuff. Her love for her family and dogs and even being passionate in counselling work showed a person who is down to earth and a joy to be around others. This holds a good ground on why she prides herself for good customer services. Her business principles in giving full assurance, best offered prices and no hard selling satisfied why she doesn't enjoy entertaining difficult customers that don't respect her pricing. All these sums up her strong belief of not being swayed easily and can be related to her faith and applying them in her life of giving back to society and yet, maintaining strong values.

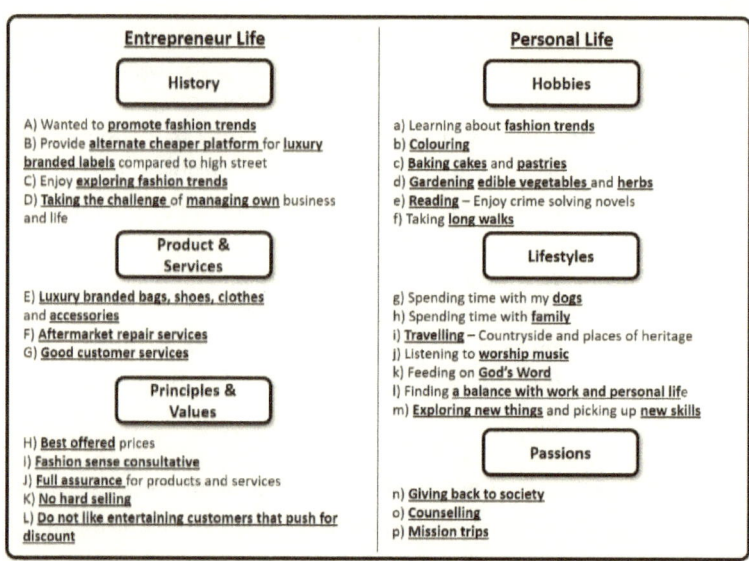

Figure 13: CLIB business model – Filled up the categories & identify keywords

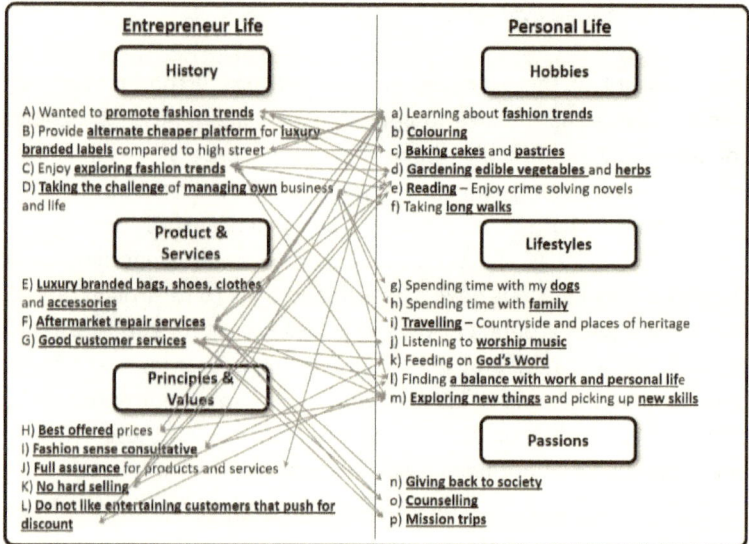

Figure 14: CLIB model for business – Cross-link the left and right items

Moving on the next step and just like the profiling snapshot, I will compare all the items on the left and right, identify the items in common and cross-linked them (see Figure 14). One thing you might have noticed is that I have removed the different levels of the categories as compared to the personal branding model. The reason is for businesses, all the categories are the summation of the whole branding, all levels are equally important to portray the complete image of the company. The approach is to personalised it but yet not making it personal. Let me elaborate on that.

Say cross-linked item Cd talks about the similarity in exploring fashion trends to that of gardening. The person probably sees exploring different methods of growing vegetables, such as studying the soils and weather conditions as a comparative exploration mindset that she also applied in assessing fashion trends. However, if she is going to be writing contents on gardening and then point out about fashion trends, people will lose focus on her business and be more interested in her gardening topic. It will be too personal from that standpoint. Because of that, instead of giving the CLIB business model a score implication approach, I created the associated outcomes approach (see Figure 15).

Cross-Linked Items	Cross-Linked Outcomes
Aa, Ab, Ac, Ae	• Promoting fashion trends
Ba, Bc	• "That" special place - Resourceful
Ca, Cd, Ce, Ci, Cm	• Trends knowledge and sharing • Learning and applying knowledge
Df, Dg, Dh, Dl	• Inspired entrepreneur
Ea, Em	• Fashion variety and options
Fa, Fd, Fe, Fn, Fo, Fp	• Reliability
Gj, Gk, Gl, Go Gp	• Relationships
Ha, Hm	• Staying competitive
Ia, Im	• Be known as the Fashion Consultant
Ja	• Trustworthy • Good shopping experience
Ka, Ke, Kk	• Shop with comfort
La, Ll	• Price assurance

Figure 15: Cross-linked items and associated outcomes

The main different in this approach compared to the score implications method is to identify the key outcomes of how the person wants his business to be through branding. The CLIB model for personal branding is focusing on cultivating the character and personality of the person. Whereas the CLIB model for business branding is focusing on cultivating the character and personality of the business. The business has to be the front instead of the business owner. But yet the business must be personalised because of the owner. Let's pick a few examples and go into deeper details.

Cross-linked example 4
"Ab" – "Promote fashion trends" vs "Colouring".

This is not a difficult cross-linked item to create a brand statement. The outcome is to promote fashion trends through understanding of colours. This can be really fun if you can put it in the right perspectives.

"When it comes to shopping for clothes, do you first look for specific fabric or colour? If you are a zealous shopper like myself, you will probably say they are both equally important.

Interestingly, I have also learned that the colours for consideration also matter on the occasions that the dressing is used for. Take the material georgette for example. Being a very thin, free flowing, silky fabric, it can be a very comfortable match for outdoor use or a summer dress. However, if it used in the day beach environment, the colour selection becomes critical. If it is in light or earthy tones, the strong sunlight glares and reflections will drain out the colour of the dress because of its thin fabric, making it looked plain and even revealing. Hence, some stronger colours in orange, red or blue will make it more stand out. Floral designs can also work well in such cases. On other hand, if that light tone dress is to be worn on the beach in the evening, the whole impression reversed. The light colours will now be more noticeable in the shades of the evening.

Hence, one of the things I always share with my clients is to think about the purpose of the apparel they are using it for. Be it work, weekends, evenings, dinners, etc. there is always a perfect fabric and colour for the occasion."

And if you are savvy in your choices, you might even find a perfect match for all kinds of occasions."

From this example, you can tell the writer is adding value by sharing insights on choosing fabrics and colours in regards to the needed occasion. At the same time, she is subtly promoting a fashion trend through the material, georgette. I bet for those who doesn't know about this material might just google it to learn more. Interestingly, she has also managed to hit a few other outcomes from this cross-linked example. She has also promoted herself delicately as a Fashion Consultant, sharing fashion knowledge and also providing fashion variety and options. Can you see how the post becomes personalised but not personal? Let's try a more challenging example.

Cross-linked example 5
"Gl" – "Good customer services" vs "a balance with work and personal life".

At a glance, you might not see any real similarity in these two items. But if you think deeper, you will realise it is about managing self before managing others. Finding time and balance for both is a skill itself. In additional to that, it shows commitment to build relationships, which was the intended outcome of this cross-linked item. Let us see how the example will be like.

"A good fashion sense without good sense in managing life will not make any good sense. That is what I always shared with my staff and clients on how I managed my life.

Being in the fashion business is not just about promoting fashion, but also in a way, promoting a lifestyle. Hence, when it comes to encouraging new fashion to the clients, I have to be the first to carry that fashion. When people see your style, they can then picture themselves better. I have always find that useful for me and my staff to strike conversations with our customers. When they see something they like in you, they get interested in you. That is always a convenience topic for discussion. From there, we learn about our customers' needs better, what kind of style and trend they are looking for. It helps us to provide better services and manage our time more effectively."

In this example, you can't find the word, "relationships" in it, but the implication is over the content. She has delicately described herself as a person who manage work and life well while at the same time, emphasis on how she builds relationships with her staff and clients. As you read the content, you can tell this person believes in good customer service and have her way of doing it. It cultivates some faith in believing her service is worth engaging. People who wants to find out more about fashions may also consider talking to her. Can you see the outcomes deriving out from this content? Many further examples can apply in this context in building relationships. You can talk about how you have helped a particular customer in her needs, the satisfaction from seeing her customer getting what she wanted and even her good advice that helped a customer's fashion dilemma.

Cross-linked example 6
"La" – "Do not like entertaining customers that push for discount" vs "fashion trends".

For the last example, let's try a more challenging one. The outcome of this match is price assurance. Talking about money in contents are always not easy, especially when you want to promote the value that your prices are competitive. In this aspect, the person faces struggling occasions where demanding clients push for discounts. No business owners will enjoy such clients who don't appreciate the value of your products and services. But when you establish a good brand, people can respect your price. So, let's see how this expectation can be articulated through a content.

"When it comes to a retail business like ours, the key thing my team always emphasise on is good shopping experience. It is what makes the difference between a shop with good products and a shop worth shopping at.

But like any retail businesses, we have our fair share of challenges to please every customer. Every shopper including myself will always enjoy a good bargain. However, because the business relies on a lot of regular customers, we also tried to manage them in spending. The last thing we want is they start overspending and then stop visiting our boutique. Let's face it, luxury goods are always tempting and the fashion trends never end. Being practical is important. When you purchased something that is cheap but with no practical use, it ends up as expensive. Especially when it comes to luxury goods where the prices always stay competitive without significant deviation.

Hence, we always aim to ensure our customers purchased goods that are value for money in terms of their needs and usage. We believe the real joy of shopping is after you used your products and experienced it. That's how we keep our customers happy."

This post emphasises a lot on being practical and ensure the customers can remain satisfied in their purchases. The outcomes come with many facets which include reliability, relationships, trustworthy, good shopping experience, shop with comfort and most importantly, price assurance. The whole content centred on customer experience and assured them that. When people read this, they can respect her price assurance. In a nice subtle way, she put across her message to achieve that outcome. Again, many similar styles of content can derive from this cross-linked item. Things like customer experience after using the product, the functionality of a product and its purposes and even during promotion.

As you can see from the above examples how all the categories can become the summation of the whole branding for a business. The heartbeat of the owner resonates into the rhyme of how the business will be operated and songs are written to echo all that. In summary, the following are the 7 steps for the CLIB business model:

Step 1: Prepared your own preferred writing materials, be in pen and paper or excel spreadsheet. On the left side, list your entrepreneur life's categories of A) history, B) product & services and C) principles & values. On the right side, created your personal life's categories of a) hobbies, b) lifestyles and c) passions.

Step 2: Fill up these categories with related items as much as possible.

Step 3: Highlight all the keywords in the items.

Step 4: Compare the items between the entrepreneur life vs personal life.

Step 5: Cross-link the items.

Step 6: List out the cross-linked items onto a table and identified the associated outcomes to be achieved.

Step 7: Looked into cross-linked items and build the contents.

One aspect of the business model is the contents can get richer over time. Unlike the personal branding model where the contents can weight by the score implications and depend very much on the cross-linked item's focus, the business model is always telling stories that sum up a big portion of the business brand. Like all the big brands, followers will get to know the business better and appreciate how it operates. When you have achieved positioning your business in that way, you will have achieved a good business branding. In another aspect like what my clients did, this model can be further cultivated into business strategies. By understanding their business concept better, they can develop more focus business plans.

12.

Developing your Brand Weapon

Developing your Brand Weapon

Now that you have learned everything essential from content writing to cracking the social media algorithms, the final question is how to combine all of them and build your branding. And this is what this chapter is all about. At the end of the day, you need to develop your personalised brand weapon and know how to swing it well into good hits. To make this easy for you, I have come up a step-by-step game plan to show you how to use your brand weapon effectively. Consider this like playing a computer game.

Step 1: Create your fortress.

Like any gaming, in order to begin, you need to build a strong fortress or castle first. This is the place where people identified you. Yes, this is your Facebook / LinkedIn profile, page or group. Choose nice pictures for your background and get a professional profile photo. Give a well thought summary of your profile and share what values you can offer. This is your virtual shop. When people walk into that shop, they must get a good vide and enjoy touring around. When they leave, they must gain a good impression of you. When people keep returning to visit your shop, then it shows your brand is drawing people.

Step 2: Build your ammunition box(es).

Once you created your CLIB model, don't rush into publishing every content you wrote right away. Have a strategy plan. Don't go into battle without enough ammunition. My advice is to build as many contents as you can before posting. You need to have enough bullets that can last at least 2-3 weeks ahead. Once you completed your contents, look at them again and see if you can refine them. Personally, I believe a picture can say a thousand words. Hence, think of suitable pictures that can go with your contents. To date, my CLIB model has enabled me to prepare contents for my daily posts that can last for more than a year.

This approach is important because once you open up your virtual shop, people will get hungry for more. You have to keep feeding them. You can't run out of supply. Consistency is the key. If you stop posting for prolong period, people lose interest in you and you have to take more efforts to reignite those fire in them.

Step 3: Identify your target group.

Once you have your ammunitions ready, the next thing is to find and identify your targets. As you write your contents, you will start to realise who are your potential viewers. Using the algorithms that I taught in previous chapters, look for similar interest groups and people to connect. Get them into your sight. Have your sniper scope all pointing at them.

Step 4: Line up your targets and choose your timing.

When you got your targets in sight and your ammunitions ready. Line them up and choose your timing carefully. Your contents must be flexible. A mistake that one of my students made is writing the same cross-linked item and keep posting the similar stuff. People get bored over time with the same kind of story and the worst thing is they don't know what else to comment further. Hence, you need to change your content position and target at different angles.

Step 5: Keep firing.

As I mentioned, consistency is important. When you start hitting your targets, you shouldn't be stopping. You should keep firing and keep them on the move. Get them to respond, get them into actions. When you turned yourself into a hot zone, this is when your branding starts to rise exponentially.

Step 6: Grenades & landmines.

What happened when your targets are coming at your contents? You are now a hot zone and people are dancing wild, what else can you do? It is time to throw grenades and plan landmines. Take out your best contents, articles and promotions to drive them crazy. Made fireworks and enjoy the ripples!

Step 7: Gain allies

Along the journey of branding, you will meet friends and foes. You will encounter people who are nasty in their comments while there are also very nice humble friends to make. Choose your battle wisely and make the right friends. These friends can become your powerful allies to sustain your brand.

The above is my simple seven steps game plan that I have used to teach my students and clients to launch their brand weapons. Most of them stick by it but of course some of them alter the steps to suit their needs and routines. The point is nothing is cast in stone and you have to find the game plan that works for you.

13. Setting your KPIs

Setting your KPIs

I believe in Key Performance Indicators (KPIs). Without that, you will not know where you stand in your branding and how well you have performed. You will not know what kind of results are considered good if you don't set your own objectives. Let's face it, social media branding does require some amount of time and effort. If you don't measure your results, you will not be able to see what you want to see and eventually grew tired and give up. Hence, you need to set some KPIs for yourself. However, this chapter is not to tell you exactly what KPIs to follow, you have to learn to personalise what you want to achieve. Instead, I am going to give you some pointers to develop your own KPIs in branding.

Let's start with lifestyle social media platform on personal use and branding. Virtually, I do believe the amount of likes and comments you received in your posts do reveal at certain level, your popularity among your friends. If you hardly receive any, there are typical three reasons for that. Either 1) your posts are filled with negativity, 2) you don't take interest or engage in other people's posts or 3) you are generally not well liked as a person (being honest here). Hence, if you want to gain popularity among your friends, these are the three areas to work on. In my own experience, there is a rough guide on what kind of results will consider a person is popular among his friends. Consider he has 500 connections and if he has an average of 50 likes per post, then he is likely to be in the popular range. Typically, in any social media account, ~50% of the connections are not really active regular users, ~25% of the connections will be normal perusing users with little engagement and only ~25% are serious active social media users. Hence, if you can attract around 10-25% active engagement from your number of connections, you are generally a good friend to stay in contact virtually. Of course, this guide is just based on statistical analytic data of users and market research done. If you are only starting to build your personal branding, you have to give yourself around 2 to 3 months to see some stable results.

If you are using lifestyle social media platform for business purposes, do refer back to the section above. Because if you don't know how to connect well with friends, you are not likely able to connect well in the business platform. Firstly, you need some friends to give support to your business. Secondly, if you haven't learned how to gain popularity in your virtual personal life, you will not achieve much success in the same department for your virtual business. You will realise most online social media business users characteristically have some interestingly personalities. Hence, using the above calculation, you will know how much engagement you can get from your followers. However, do take note in business platform, the number of reaches from connections are more critical. Therefore, I will suggest putting your followers to more than 25k as one of your KPIs. A decent group engagement is typical 1 to 3% of the total number of connections. When you can hit around this range, you should then see how much of that percentage is converted into business. That ratio is what you have to work on.

In the likes of professional social media platform, if you applied the algorithms and content strategies well, you will probably see some good results as fast as a month's time. Your typical posts will generally start off with daily 30 to 50 counts of likes and comments. Generally, a post that can hit more than 100 counts of likes and many constructive comments is considered a popular post. But at the end of the day, that is not the final KPI. Your true KPIs should relate to how often you are approached for job and business opportunities. In that aspect and just like lifestyle social media platforms, you have to consider how much effort you put in for the traditional way of networking. Do you connect with people virtually but never make an effort to have a cup of coffee? How often you reach out to give someone a helping hand? The real relationships come from these engagements and to me, that is the real KPI on the level of personal branding that defines your character and personality. So work on that!

14. Closing Words

Closing Words

Dear reader, we have come to an end of this book and it has been a privilege for me to share my thoughts and experience with you. I hoped you have gained new perspectives and insights from this book on hopefully develop your own powerful brand weapon. If time permit that one day our path should ever cross in one way or another, and if you ever visit Singapore, do reach out to me. I will love to meet up with you and show you around in my beautiful country.

If you like to check on my future posts, you may also follow me on LinkedIn at https://www.linkedin.com/in/glennleehg/. Drop me a message and hopefully we can build our relationship from there.

#GlennDailyWisdom - My daily sharing from my life experience using quotes that I researched. The intent is to encourage and motivate readers in life and at work. (Posting time ~8am Singapore).

#GlennHumorForABreak - All work and no play makes Glenn a dull boy. Apart from the serious stuff, a bit of humour can lighten up someone's life. This is another of my daily sharing. Post after 5pm (Singapore time), so that people can enjoy some humour after work.

#GlennHopeGrace - Spiritual sharing which I posted only on Sundays. I try not to reply on comments on this post but let God takes the glory.

#GlennCorporateStories – Wonderful sharing of work life experience that is worth keeping as a good memory and reminder. No definite schedule.

Cheers and stay blessed always!

www.ingramcontent.com/pod-product-compliance
Lightning Source LLC
Chambersburg PA
CBHW020446220526
45464CB00002B/875